Weather Sense
Temperature, Air Pressure, and Wind

Author
Ann Wiebe

Illustrator
Margo Pocock

Editor
Betty Cordel

Desktop Publisher
Tanya Adams

Meteorological Consultant
Lawrence Greiss
National Weather Service
Hanford, California

Acknowledgments

Initial Idea Team
John Carmean
Betty Cordel
Dan Freeman
Tom Kelly
Linda Stansfield

Additional Technical Illustrations
Michelle Pauls

This book contains materials developed by the AIMS Education Foundation. **AIMS** (**A**ctivities **I**ntegrating **M**athematics and **S**cience) began in 1981 with a grant from the National Science Foundation. The non-profit AIMS Education Foundation publishes hands-on instructional materials (books and the monthly magazine) that integrate curricular disciplines such as mathematics, science, language arts, and social studies. The Foundation sponsors a national program of professional development through which educators may gain both an understanding of the AIMS philosophy and expertise in teaching by integrated, hands-on methods.

ISBN **1-881431-96-7**
Printed in the United States of America

Weather Sense
Temperature, Air Pressure, Wind
Table of Contents

Introduction

As we wake in the morning, our thoughts turn to the day ahead. We peek out the window, read the paper, or turn on a newscast. Do I need a coat today? A scarf or mittens? An umbrella? Sunscreen? Will school start late because of fog or snow? Will the baseball game be cancelled due to rain? Weather affects people of all ages.

Children experience weather on a very personal level. It is tangible; it is relevant to their lives. This atmospheric laboratory is always present and available to tap their curiosity, whether testing the truth of historical proverbs (the earliest weather forecasters), measuring weather elements, or making sense of weather patterns.

Weather Sense: Temperature, Air Pressure, and Wind and its companion publication, *Weather Sense: Moisture,* are built around direct observation at a local site. Students will discover evidence of the unequal heating of Earth, the big idea behind weather, as they begin a lifetime journey toward comprehending why this is so. On the first level, attention is given to the particular key question in the activity being investigated. On the next level, the outcome of the investigation is related to the bigger essential question that drives a section of study. At an even higher level, it is hoped students will begin to relate the elements of weather—temperature, air pressure, wind, moisture—to each other. As they navigate through middle school and beyond, understanding the complexities of weather will involve connecting the physical sciences (heat energy, force and motion) and the earth sciences (solar system) and geography.

The ocean of air surrounding Earth is constantly on the move, but not always predictable. A barely perceptible change in one variable can ripple through the atmosphere, triggering a shift from the expected to the unexpected—from warm to cool, from breezy to gale force, from dry to wet. Weather can be harsh, but it can also be beautiful. It is cause for wonder.

> When we contemplate the whole globe as one great dewdrop, striped and dotted with continents and islands, flying through space with all the other stars, all singing and shining together as one, the whole universe appears as an infinite storm of beauty. This grand show is eternal. It is always sunrise somewhere; the dew is never all dried at once; a shower is forever falling; vapor ever rising. Eternal sunrise, eternal sunset, eternal dawn and gloaming, on seas and continents and islands, each in its turn, as the round earth rolls.
>
> John Muir (1838-1914) from *My First Summer in the Sierra*

The Big Picture

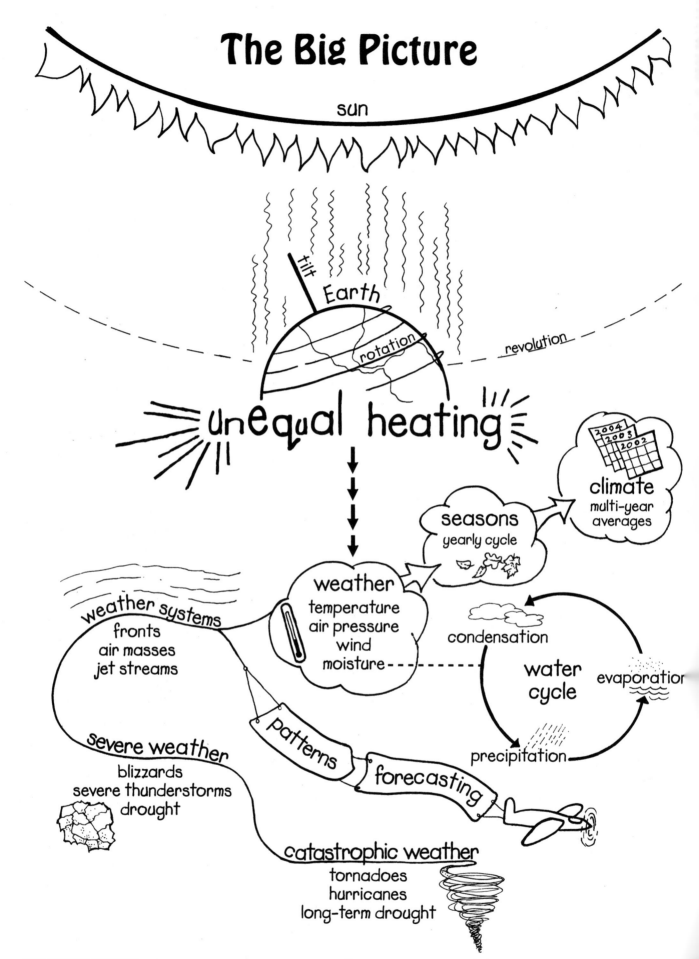

sun

tilt

Earth

rotation

revolution

unEqual heating

seasons
yearly cycle

climate
multi-year
averages

weather
temperature
air pressure
wind
moisture

condensation

water
cycle

evaporation

weather systems
fronts
air masses
jet streams

precipitation

patterns

forecasting

severe weather
blizzards
severe thunderstorms
drought

catastrophic weather
tornadoes
hurricanes
long-term drought

Weather Close Up

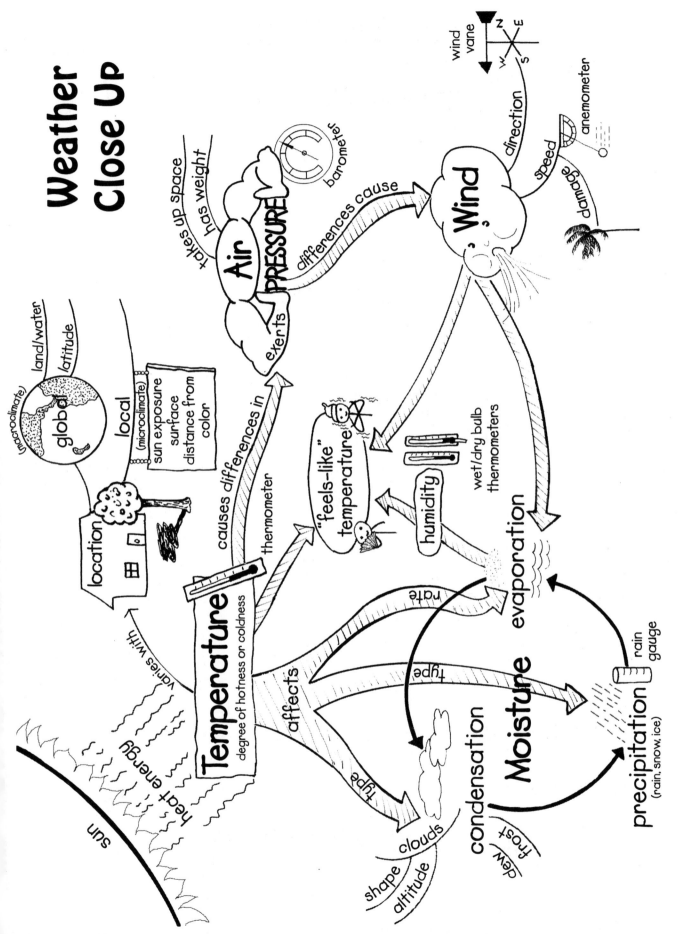

Weather Sense
Learning Goals

Investigate how the unequal heating of the Earth drives weather—temperature, air pressure, wind, and moisture.

- Observe and gather evidence that temperature varies with location, both locally and globally.

- Observe and gather evidence of the properties of air, the medium in which weather exists.

- Observe and gather evidence that wind varies in direction and speed.

- Observe and gather evidence that water endlessly cycles through evaporation (humidity), condensation (clouds and dew), and precipitation (rain and snow), causing a variety of weather conditions.

- Construct and/or use meteorological tools, such as thermometers, psychrometers, anemometers, and barometers, to quantify observations.

- Determine daily, weekly, and seasonal weather patterns for your location.

- Begin to understand how the four elements of weather—temperature, air pressure, wind, and moisture—interact with each other.

More specific learning goals for the individual weather elements are found on the assessment pages.

National Education Reform Documents

The AIMS Education Foundation is committed to remaining at the cutting edge of providing curriculum materials that are user-friendly, educationally sound, developmentally appropriate, and aligned with the recommendations found in national education reform documents.

NRC Standards*

Science as Inquiry
- *Plan and conduct a simple investigation.*
- *Employ simple equipment and tools to gather data and extend the senses.*
- *Use appropriate tools and techniques to gather, analyze, and interpret data.*
- *Use data to construct a reasonable explanation.*
- *Communicate investigations and explanations.*
- *Scientists develop explanations using observations (evidence) and what they already know about the world (scientific knowledge). Good explanations are based on evidence from investigations.*

Physical Science
- *Objects have many observable properties, including size, weight, shape, color, temperature, and the ability to react with other substances. Those properties can be measured using tools, such as rulers, balances, and thermometers.*
- *The position and motion of objects can be changed by pushing or pulling. The size of the change is related to the strength of the push or pull.*

Earth and Space Science
- *Earth materials are solid rocks and soil, water, and the gases of the atmosphere. The varied materials have different physical and chemical properties, which make them useful in different ways, for example, as building materials, as sources of fuel, or for growing the plants we use as food. Earth materials provide many of the resources that humans use.*
- *The sun provides the light and heat necessary to maintain the temperature of the earth.*
- *Weather changes from day to day and over the seasons. Weather can be described by measurable quantities, such as temperature, wind direction and speed, and precipitation.*

Science and Technology
- *Tools help scientists make better observations, measurements, and equipment for investigations. They help scientists see, measure, and do things that they could not otherwise see, measure, and do.*

Science in Personal and Social Perspectives
- *Safety and security are basic needs of humans. Safety involves freedom from danger, risk, or injury. Security involves feelings of confidence and lack of anxiety and fear. Student understandings include following safety rules for home and school, preventing abuse and neglect, avoiding injury, knowing whom to ask for help, and when and how to say no.*

* National Research Council. *National Science Education Standards.* National Academy Press. Washington D.C. 1996.

Project 2061 Benchmarks*

The Nature of Science
- *Scientific investigations may take many different forms, including observing what things are like or what is happening somewhere, collecting specimens for analysis, and doing experiments. Investigations can focus on physical, biological, and social questions.*
- *Scientists' explanations about what happens in the world come partly from what they observe, partly from what they think. Sometimes scientists have different explanations for the same set of observations. That usually leads to their making more observations to resolve the differences.*

The Nature of Technology
- *Measuring instruments can be used to gather accurate information for making scientific comparisons of objects and events and for designing and constructing things that will work properly.*

The Physical Setting
- *The sun warms the land, air, and water.*
- *Air is a substance that surrounds us, takes up space, and whose movement we feel as wind.*
- *Some materials conduct heat much better than others. Poor conductors can reduce heat loss.*

The Mathematical World
- *In some situations, "0" means none of something, but in others it may be just the label of some point on a scale.*
- *When people care about what is being counted or measured, it is important for them to say what the units are (three degrees Fahrenheit is different from three centimeters, three miles from three miles per hour).*
- *If 0 and 1 are located on a line, any other number can be depicted as a position on the line.*
- *Graphical display of numbers may make it possible to spot patterns that are not otherwise obvious, such as comparative size and trends.*

Common Themes
- *Geometric figures, number sequences, graphs, diagrams, sketches, number lines, maps, and stories can be used to represent objects, events, and processes in the real world, although such representations can never be exact in every detail.*
- *Things change in steady, repetitive, or irregular ways—or sometimes in more than one way at the same time. Often the best way to tell which kinds of change are happening is to make a table or graph of measurements.*

Habits of Mind
- *Offer reasons for their findings and consider reasons suggested by others.*
- *Add, subtract, multiply, and divide whole numbers mentally, on paper, and with a calculator.*
- *Keep a notebook that describes observations made, carefully distinguishes actual observations from ideas and speculations about what was observed, and is understandable weeks or months later.*
- *Make sketches to aid in explaining procedures or ideas.*
- *Use numerical data in describing and comparing objects and events.*
- *Recognize when comparisons might not be fair because some conditions are not kept the same.*

* American Association for the Advancement of Science. *Benchmarks for Science Literacy.* Oxford University Press. New York. 1993.

NCTM Standards 2000*

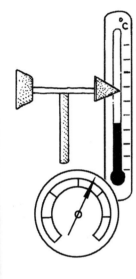

Number and Operations
- *Explore numbers less than 0 by extending the number line and through familiar applications*
- *Develop fluency in adding, subtracting, multiplying, and dividing whole numbers*

Algebra
- *Describe, extend, and make generalizations about geometric and numeric patterns*
- *Identify and describe situations with constant or varying rates of change and compare them*

Geometry
- *Describe location and movement using common language and geometric vocabulary*

Measurement
- *Understand such attributes as length, area, weight, volume, and size of angle and select the appropriate type of unit for measuring each attribute*
- *Understand the need for measuring with standard units and become familiar with standard units in the customary and metric systems*
- *Understand that measurements are approximations and understand how differences in units affect precision*
- *Select and apply appropriate standard units and tools to measure length, area, volume, weight, time, temperature, and the size of angles*
- *Select and use benchmarks to estimate measurements*

Data Analysis and Probability
- *Design investigations to address a question and consider how data-collection methods affect the nature of the data set*
- *Collect data using observations, surveys, and experiments*
- *Represent data using tables and graphs such as line plots, bar graphs, and line graphs*
- *Describe the shape and important features of a set of data and compare related data sets, with an emphasis on how the data are distributed*

Representation
- *Use representations to model and interpret physical, social, and mathematical phenomena*

* Reprinted with permission from *Principles and Standards for School Mathematics*, 2000 by the National Council of Teachers of Mathematics. All rights reserved.

National Geography Standards*

The World in Spatial Terms
- *Show spatial information on geographic representations*
- *Obtain information on the characteristics of places (e.g., climate, elevation, and population density) by interpreting maps*

* Geography Education Standards Project. *Geography for Life: National Geography Standards 1994.* National Geographic Research & Exploration. Washington, D.C. 1994.

Management Overview

A Suggested Plan

The study of weather is too complex to be accomplished in a couple of weeks; it involves much more than taking a few measurements or addressing a few highlights. Students deserve the opportunity to study weather in depth—to look for evidence of change, to become proficient with different measuring tools, to grasp the variables involved, to acquire a greater appreciation of our world—and that requires learning over time.

As such, consider studying weather over the course of the year. Rather than to present the entire unit at one time, one suggestion is to introduce weather at the beginning of the year, then intersperse other curricular units with the various weather topics as shown below. Have students continue to gather weather data at a regular time each day throughout the year.

Station Model

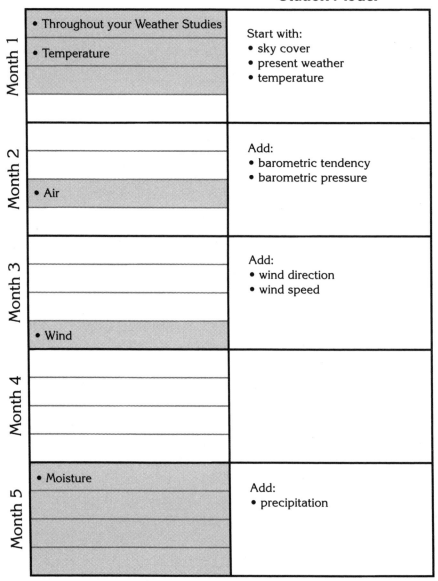

Assessment

Presenting opportunities for children to become actively engaged in learning is not enough. What do children know and what are they able to do? What naive conceptions are still held about the subject at hand? Which process skills have been mastered and which continue to be troublesome? One of the purposes of assessment is to inform instruction in order to more effectively meet the specific needs of your students. Layers of assessment are offered in *Weather Sense*.

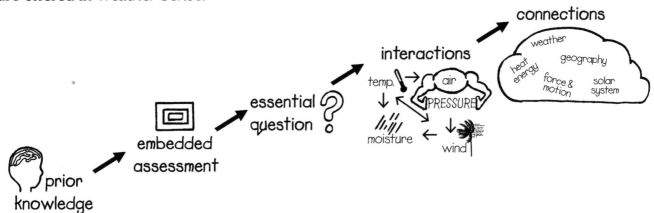

Constructing and assessing knowledge

Assessment of prior knowledge

Before embarking on any topic, it makes sense to find out what students already know. "Weather" is a rather broad subject for this task. Instead, invite students to respond to "temperature" as you prepare to study that weather element, then later to "air," "wind," and "moisture." The KWL acronym can be a helpful format for framing learning.

Things we think we know	Things we would like to know	Things we learned

Embedded assessment

Another layer is the embedded assessment which happens within an activity. Through observation of the degree of engagement, through observation of process skills being used, through questioning, and through listening to student conversations with each other, teachers are constantly assessing acquisition of concepts and skills and adapting the flow of the activity accordingly. Puzzlement about a procedure and certain conceptual questions can be dealt with immediately. Other questions may be more appropriately deferred until more knowledge has been acquired, but should be given value by being added to a class list. These observations may be informal or they may be more formally noted in an observation log. The intent of the log may be to evaluate *conceptual understanding* or it may be to assess *values, attitudes, and skills*, sometimes referred to as habits of mind.

Some activities incorporate a performance assessment within them. *A Matter of Degrees,* for example, checks progress in interpreting scales. Others, such as *On Location* and *Proverb Proofs*, can be used as performance assessments if students have had sufficient prior experiences in controlling variables and designing an investigation, respectively.

Essential question

Weather Sense, in two companion publications, is built around the four fundamental elements of weather: temperature, air pressure, wind, and moisture. Each of these elements has a corresponding essential question, a question that addresses the conceptual focus of that unit. These questions are featured in the Table of Contents and on the assessment pages. When the study of a weather element commences, display the appropriate essential question in the room. As each activity comes to a close, what has been learned that day should be related back to the essential question. The goal is for specific learning to be connected to the bigger picture.

Within each weather section is also an assessment which more formally addresses the essential question or big idea. Sometimes the assessment is in the form of suggestions and sometimes it is supported by pages that can be copied.

Journals and/or portfolios are another way for students to demonstrate their thinking and learning as is mind mapping*, a visual/symbolic concept map. Also consider having students do a self-assessment, such the partial example below, based on items you have devised.

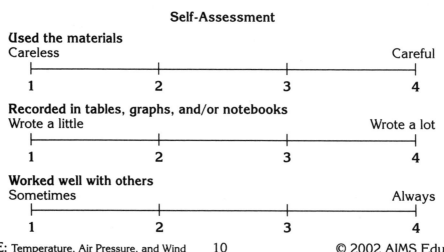

Self-Assessment

Used the materials
Careless   Careful

| 1 | 2 | 3 | 4 |

Recorded in tables, graphs, and/or notebooks
Wrote a little   Wrote a lot

| 1 | 2 | 3 | 4 |

Worked well with others
Sometimes   Always

| 1 | 2 | 3 | 4 |

Interactions

At the next level of conceptual development, the goal is for students to understand how one element of weather interacts with another. Some of the activity questions begin to probe these connections on an observational level, but there is no formal assessment here since students are just beginning to construct these connections.

Connections

Eventually students should understand the connections between weather and the other sciences—the solar system (earth science), heat energy and force and motion (physical science)—as well as geography. This does not happen in one year. The conceptual seeds that are planted as a result of doing these activities will make this goal more possible as students move through middle school, high school, and even college. Students are on a learning journey; it is constructive; it is developmental. We may never see the resulting fruit, but we will know we had a part in its growth.

Journals

A journal is a useful method for personal communication between teacher and student as well as a tool for assessing learning progress. From the standpoint of integrating the curriculum, the weather activities give a meaningful context for writing and illustration. A journal cover, near the front of this book, can be copied for student use. Suggestions for the journal include:

Visual	Written
diagram	response to a prompt or question
picture	description of a weather event
table/graph	comparison of two objects or events
map	interview
mind map*	composition of an original poem
	description of a walk on a ____ day
	(hot, windy, rainy, etc.)
	response to a non-fiction/fiction weather book

If you wish for students to have a hybrid mix of journal and portfolio, have them construct a folder. Include both journal entries and selected activity pages showing data collection, graphing, and descriptions of weather patterns.

* Margulies, Nancy. *Mapping Inner Space: Learning and Teaching Mind Mapping.* Zephyr Press. Tucson, Arizona. 1991.

Metric or Not?

The standard used by most of the world and of scientists—and you and your class are practicing scientists—is the metric system. This includes the National Weather Service meteorologists (U.S.), although they presently report data in customary units. If at all possible, you are encouraged to obtain equipment and make measurements in metric units.

If metric measuring tools are not available, use those you have. Students should not be asked to convert from one system to the other. Records and graphs should reflect the system with which measurements were made. However, on those rare occasions when student measurements are going to be directly compared with official meteorological measurements, such as in *Temperature Tally,* use the corresponding units of measurement.

A Word about Weather Stations

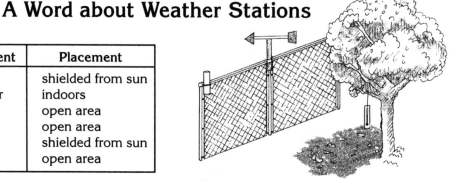

Weather Station Instrument	Placement
thermometer	shielded from sun
balloon/aneroid barometer	indoors
wind vane	open area
anemometer	open area
sling psychrometer	shielded from sun
rain gauge	open area

As the activities in these books are explored, several homemade weather instruments will be constructed. These include a balloon barometer for detecting air pressure changes, a wind vane for wind direction, an anemometer to measure wind speed, a sling psychrometer for relative humidity, and a rain gauge. These instruments, along with a thermometer, are intended to be taken outdoors at specified times and returned indoors after measurements are completed. The exceptions are the barometer, which requires the more controlled environment found indoors, and the rain gauge, which will need to stay outside for the duration of a storm.

A permanent weather station with homemade instruments is not generally feasible at a school site for several reasons. First, the homemade instruments are more fragile than commercial ones and may not be sturdy enough to withstand the variations of weather day in and day out. Second, they would need to be set up in an open area away from buildings and trees. This can be problematic since the school playground is used for so many activities and often by the community after hours. Third, to protect the thermometer from the sun, a Stevenson screen would need to be built. This box is made of wood, has vents, and is painted white, along with other specifications. A cardboard version would disintegrate in wet weather.

If you are keenly interested in a permanent weather station, commercial ones are available. Sometimes local television stations are willing to offer help in financing this effort, with an eye toward using your weather data—in addition to their own sources. Also contact community groups for financial support.

I Hear and I Forget,

I See and
I Remember,

I Do
and I
Understand.

Chinese Proverb

Weather
Journal

Global Weather Extremes

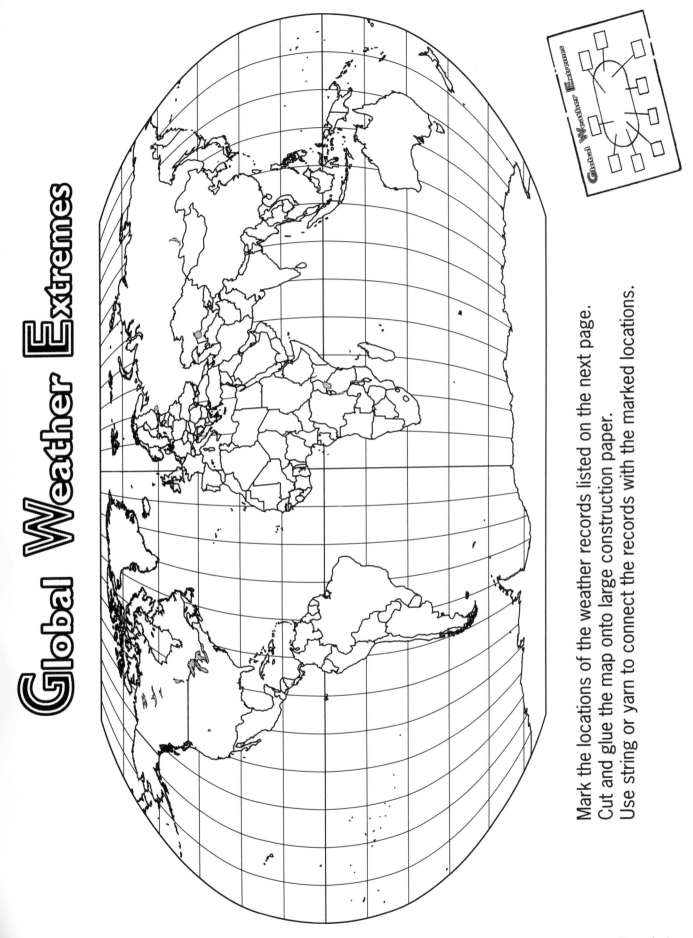

Mark the locations of the weather records listed on the next page.
Cut and glue the map onto large construction paper.
Use string or yarn to connect the records with the marked locations.

Global Weather Extremes

Use some or all of these records on the map.

Highest Temperature
58°C (136°F)
El Azizia, Libya (32°N 13°E)
September 13, 1922

Lowest Temperature
-89°C (-129°F)
Vostok, Antarctica (72°S 13°E)
July 21, 1983

Highest Air Pressure
1084 mb (32 in)
Agata, Siberia, Russia
(66°N 92°E)
December 31, 1968

Lowest Air Pressure
868 mb (25.63 in)
Typhoon Tip
(17°N 138°E, Pacific Ocean)
October 12, 1979

Highest Wind Gust
(directly measured)
372 km/h (231 mph)
Mt. Washington, New Hampshire
April 12, 1934

Highest Wind Gust
(remotely measured)
512 km/h (318 mph)
F5 tornado in Moore, Oklahoma
(suburb of Oklahoma City)
May 3, 1999

Highest Annual Average Rainfall
1187.2 cm (467.4 in)
Mawsynram, India (25°N 91°E)
(38-year span)

1168.4 cm (460.0 in)
Mt. Waialeale, Kauai, Hawaii
(32-year span)

Either of these may have the record, depending on
measurement practices and period of record variations.

Lowest Annual Average Rainfall
0.08 cm (0.03 in)
Arica, Chile (18°S 69°W)
(59-year span)

Highest Annual Total Rainfall
2644 cm (1041 in)
Cherrapunji, India (25°N 91°E)
August 1860-July 1861

Highest 24-hour Rainfall
187 cm (73.62 in)
Cilaos, Reunion Island
(21°S 56°E, South Indian Ocean)
March 15-16, 1952

Highest Annual Snowfall
289.6 cm (1140 in)
Mt. Baker, Washington
1998-1999

A Matter of DEGREES

Topic
Measurement: reading weather instrument scales

Key Question
How can we measure more precisely?

Focus
Students will determine the number patterns on a variety of scales (number lines), then apply this knowledge to measuring and graphing assorted temperatures. A different scale (barometer) will be used for assessment.

Guiding Documents
Project 2061 Benchmarks
- *Measuring instruments can be used to gather accurate information for making scientific comparisons of objects and events and for designing and constructing things that will work properly.*
- *In some situations, "0" means none of something, but in others it may be just the label of some point on a scale.*
- *If 0 and 1 are located on a line, any other number can be depicted as a position on the line.*
- *When people care about what is being counted or measured, it is important for them to say what the units are (three degrees Fahrenheit is different from three centimeters, three miles from three miles per hour).*

NRC Standard
- *Tools help scientists make better observations, measurements, and equipment for investigations. They help scientists see, measure, and do things that they could not otherwise see, measure, and do.*

NCTM Standards 2000*
- *Explore numbers less than 0 by extending the number line and through familiar applications*
- *Describe, extend, and make generalizations about geometric and numeric patterns*
- *Understand the need for measuring with standard units and become familiar with standard units in the customary and metric systems*
- *Understand that measurements are approximations and understand how differences in units affect precision*
- *Collect data using observations, surveys, and experiments*

Math
Number patterns
Estimation
Measurement
    temperature
Bar graph

Science
Earth science
    meteorology

Integrated Processes
Observing
Collecting and recording data
Comparing and contrasting
Applying

Materials
12" x 18" construction paper, 1 white and 1 red
    (see *Management 1*)
Glue
Several thermometers
Transparencies (see *Management 2*)
Toothpicks
Scissors, optional

Background Information
Procedures for precise measurement

    Scales, a practical application of the number line, are the basis of many of the measuring tools that we encounter in our daily lives—from speedometers, to rulers, to thermometers. *Since the increments on scales vary, they need to be determined.* Many, such as a thermometer, are marked in 1- or 2-unit intervals. Others, like a graduated cylinder, may jump by fives, twenties, or even hundreds. Still others are marked with parts of a whole unit (decimals), such as a rain gauge in inches; this may be because the chosen unit is large and/or very small quantities need to be measured.

    To gather meaningful data, the *unit of measurement must be identified* and labeled. This unit is usually derived from one of two measuring systems, customary or metric. Thermometers may have a Celsius or Fahrenheit scale. A rain gauge scale may be in millimeters or inches. Even more unit choices are associated with barometers: centimeters, inches, millibars, or kilopascals.

Another procedure leading toward more precise measurement is to *read the scale at eye level*, in other words, with eyes perpendicular to the measuring device. Angles other than perpendicular result in a distorted observation.

Measurement readings benefit from *careful, rather than hurried, observation of the indicator, level of liquid, etc.* Sometimes a measuring instrument, such as a thermometer, also needs to be given time to register the conditions which it is measuring before a useful reading can be taken.

The need for precise measuring skills crosses through many disciplines of mathematics and science. A study of scale also connects to graphing, both in construction, where the increment chosen has a direct effect on the way the data look, and in interpretation of data, which is dependent on recognizing the increments being used. Yet students are often not taught, or are assumed to have already acquired, the necessary skills. Determine the prior knowledge of students in evaluating whether to proceed.

Approximation of measurement

Measurements are approximate for at least three reasons. 1) Any measuring unit can be subdivided into still smaller units which are more precise. A millimeter scale is more precise than a centimeter scale. But millimeters can be further divided into tenths and those tenths can be divided into tenths and so on. 2) A measurement reading is somewhat subjective, in that the observer estimates the indicator's placement in relation to a scale; it may not be exactly at one of the scale lines. The greater the jump between increments, the more challenging the estimation becomes. Rounding to a specified unit, whether a degree or a centimeter, also results in an approximation. The larger the unit, the greater the approximation. 3) The quality and accuracy of measuring instruments vary. The measuring instruments research scientists use are more accurately callibrated and more sensitive to minute changes than the inexpensive tools generally available in schools.

Weather instruments

Scales abound in weather instruments. In the *Weather Sense* books, a thermometer will be used to measure temperature, a barometer for air pressure, a protractor and chart for wind speed, a rain gauge for rainfall totals, and a sling psychrometer with wet- and dry-bulb thermometers for relative humidity. The use of metric units is recommended in most activities, as it is the language of scientists and most of the world. Although the National Weather Service in the United States still reports temperature in degrees Fahrenheit, their measurements are taken in degrees Celsius (in conformance with international meteorological standards) and then converted.

Management

1. To make the thermometer bands, cut the construction paper into six-inch widths. Glue a red sheet to a white sheet, overlapping about $\frac{1}{2}$ inch along the 18-inch edges. When dry, cut into $\frac{1}{4}$-inch widths. Each student will need one band.

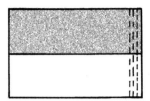

2. Transparencies of the activity pages, used on the overhead projector, are helpful for instructing about scales, modeling thermometer procedure, and for showing data results. To make a transparent thermometer band, cut a $\frac{1}{4}$-inch strip from the edge of the transparency and color half of it with a red marker.

3. This activity has three parts: practice in identifying and numbering scales, hands-on experience with a thermometer, and assessment with a barometer scale. Use the thermometer page (1- or 2-degree increments) that corresponds to your thermometers.

4. Before distributing the thermometer page, make the slits for the thermometer band with a craft knife or razor blade. Also cut slits in the matching transparency. Alternatively, students can fold the line to be slit in half and make small cuts with scissors.

5. Decide which temperature measurements will be taken. They do not need to relate to weather. Indoor examples include placing the thermometer in the center of the room, on a window ledge, inside a desk, on the floor, near the ceiling, in ice water, in hot water, or with a hand closed around the bulb.

6. If measuring in degrees Celsius, display the *Celsius Poem* so students can begin to relate common temperatures with the numbers. Water boils at 100°C and freezes at 0°C. Normal body temperature is 37°.

Procedure

Scale savvy

1. On the chalkboard or a transparency, draw the following scale:

   Ask, "What is this scale counting by?" [ones] "What numbers are missing?" [1, 2, 3] Add them to the scale. "Could there be smaller numbers in between, say, the 0 and the 1?" [Yes, $\frac{1}{2}$ or .5 and $\frac{1}{10}$ or .1, for example.] Explain that the smaller numbers would make the measurements, whatever the unit, even more precise.

   Erase the numbers and re-label the scale as shown:

   Ask, "What is this scale counting by?" [fives] "What numbers are missing?" [5, 10, 20] "Where would 13 be on this scale?" [between 10 and 15, but closer to 15] "If you were graphing using this scale, what could help you more carefully choose where 13 should be? [marking the distance between 10 and 15 into five equal spaces]

   Because scales vary, inform students that any time they use a measuring tool, they need to identify the measuring unit and the jumps, or increments, on the scale.

2. Give students the first activity page and have them record the following numbers as shown:

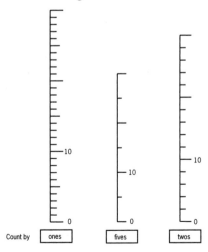

3. Direct the students' attention to the first scale. Ask, "How many marked spaces are between 1 and 10?" [10] "So each line jumps by how much?" [1] Have them write in the amount of the jump as well as the missing numbers (or at least the fives) on the scale.

Ask students to point to where 17 would be on the scale, then 6. Continue in the same manner with the other scales. "On which scale(s) was it easiest to find 17?" [probably the first scale] "How about 6?" [both the first and the third scales] "Which scale is most precise?" [the first one]

Depending on your curricular goals, another copy of this page can be used for practicing with negative numbers, decimals, and/or larger increments.

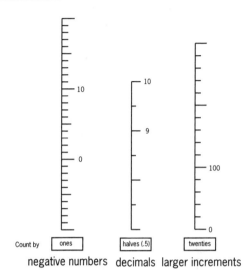

4. Encourage students to hunt for a variety of scales in the classroom and at home. See the journal prompt at the end of *Discussion*.

Hands-on experience: thermometers

1. Distribute the chosen temperature page, thermometer bands, and thermometers. Have students number both the thermometer and the graph scales at the longest lines only (tens). If Celsius is being used, the scale should start at -20° and go to 100°. For Fahrenheit, pick a range that will encompass the temperatures that students will take.

2. Instruct students about the procedures for taking precise measurements (see *Background Information*). Additional precautions specific to thermometers include keeping hands away from the bulb and reading the thermometer before removing it from the environment being measured.

   Have small groups measure the room's air temperature, slide their temperature bands through the slits, and position them to reflect their readings.

3. Share results as you walk around observing the thermometers and assessing the use of the scale. The thermometer band can be quickly repositioned, if necessary, leaving no record of mistakes.

Discuss possible reasons for temperature variations by asking, "Why might our thermometers give different measurements?" [They didn't match to start with, one place in the room might be cooler than another, they weren't read carefully, etc.] Give further instruction as needed and direct students to complete the first column of the temperature graph.

4. Encourage students to suggest (or you choose) four more temperature-taking experiences. Each measurement should be shown with the thermometer band and recorded on the graph. Completed graphs should have three labels: the title, the measuring unit (°C or °F), and the names of the five things that were measured.

5. As students engage in temperature measurement, assess their use of specific procedures for taking precise measurements: waiting for the thermometer to register the temperature, reading the scale at eye level, interpreting the scale correctly, and identifying the measurement unit (°C or °F).

Scale assessment
1. Have each student use the barometer page and a toothpick as an indicator to show measurements you say, such as 1018 millibars, 1007 millibars, and so on. The curved path provides a new twist, and the presence of two scales puts students' interpretation skills to the test. Success depends on attention to the appropriate measuring unit and identification of the scale increments.

2. Use the inch scale for additional experiences, if desired.

Discussion
1. Which is easier to read, a scale that jumps by ones or a scale that jumps by twos? [a scale that jumps by ones] Why? [You estimate more when a scale jumps by twos because some of the counting numbers are missing.]

2. Why don't all scales jump by ones? [There may not be enough room for all the lines, bigger jumps are needed when dealing with larger numbers, etc.]

3. How is *zero* on a temperature scale different from *zero* pieces of pie? [For temperature, *zero* is a label of a point on the scale but when counting pies, it means you have none.]

4. Why is it important to name the unit with which you are measuring? [Different units have different meanings. For example, 20° Celsius means the temperature is comfortable, but 20° Fahrenheit means it is colder than freezing.] What does *zero* mean on the Celsius scale? [freezing point of water] ...on the Fahrenheit scale? [colder than the freezing point of water]

5. How do the Fahrenheit and Celsius scales compare? [may have different increments, the units are not the same because the numbers across from each other don't match—10 in °C is 50 in °F]

6. Does the temperature of what you are measuring change when you switch from Celsius to Fahrenheit? [No, the temperature physically remains the same. It is just being measured by different units of heat energy.]

7. Where have you seen Celsius temperatures reported? [time and temperature signs on businesses, international weather websites, etc.]

8. Give an example of how measurement is approximate.

 Journal Prompt: Find and record as many measuring tools with scales as possible. List the measuring unit and by how much they jump. An example:

Tool	Increment	Unit
ruler	16ths	inches
ruler	10ths	centimeters
thermometer	2	degrees Celsius
thermometer	1	degrees Fahrenheit
barometer	2	millibars
barometer	20ths	inches
protractor	1	degrees
graduated cylinder	1	milliliters
spring scale	10	grams
spring scale	1	newtons
speedometer	10	miles per hour
speedometer	20	kilometers per hour
bathroom scale	1	pounds/kilograms

* Reprinted with permission from *Principles and Standards for School Mathematics*, 2000 by the National Council of Teachers of Mathematics. All rights reserved.

A Matter of DEGREES

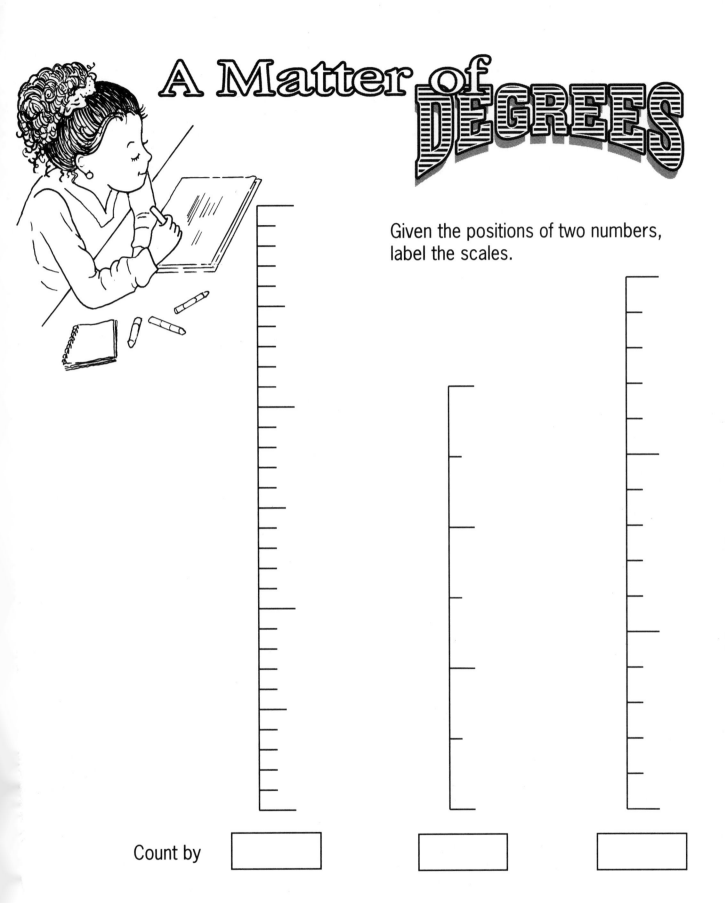

Given the positions of two numbers, label the scales.

Count by

What kinds of scales can you find?
How are they divided?
What units of measurement do they use?

A Matter of DEGREES

- Wait until the thermometer liquid stops moving.
- Read at eye level.
- Record to the nearest degree.

Show the temperature with your thermometer band.

Temperature Graph

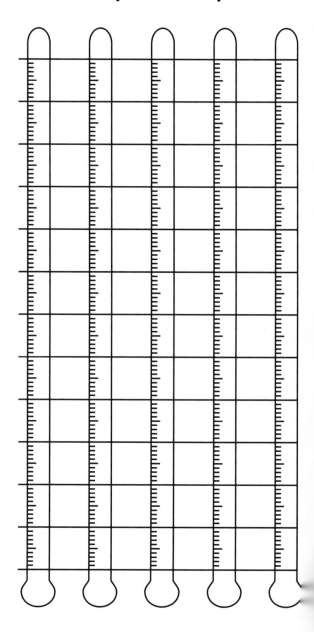

A Matter of DEGREES

- Wait until the thermometer liquid stops moving.
- Read at eye level.
- Record to the nearest degree.

Show the temperature with your thermometer band.

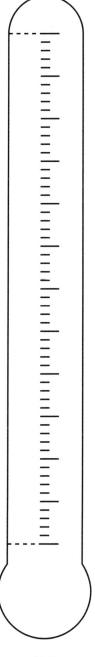

Temperature Graph

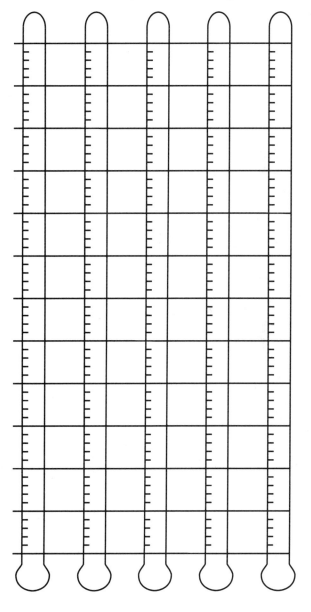

A Matter of DEGREES

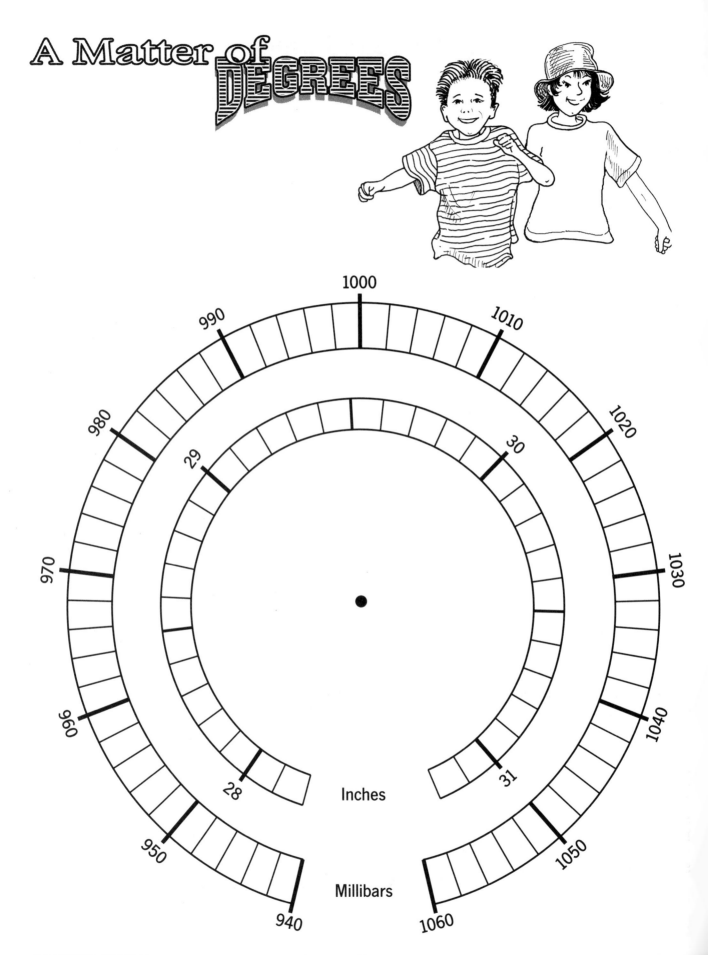

1000

990

1010

980

1020

29

30

970

1030

960

1040

950

31

1050

28

Inches

940

Millibars

1060

Proverb Proofs

Topic
Weather proverbs

Challenge
Design an investigation to test one of the weather proverbs.

Focus
Each student group will choose a weather proverb, make a plan to test its accuracy, gather data, and report conclusions.

Guiding Documents
Project 2061 Benchmarks
- *Scientific investigations may take many different forms, including observing what things are like or what is happening somewhere, collecting specimens for analysis, and doing experiments. Investigations can focus on physical, biological, and social questions.*
- *Keep a notebook that describes observations made, carefully distinguishes actual observations from ideas and speculations about what was observed, and is understandable weeks or months later.*

NRC Standards
- *Plan and conduct a simple investigation.*
- *Employ simple equipment and tools to gather data and extend the senses.*
- *Communicate investigations and explanations.*

NCTM Standards 2000*
- *Design investigations to address a question and consider how data-collection methods affect the nature of the data set*
- *Collect data using observations, surveys, and experiments*
- *Represent data using tables and graphs such as line plots, bar graphs, and line graphs*

Math (dependent on proverbs chosen and student plans)
Measurement
Graphing
Statistics

Science
Earth science
   meteorology
Scientific inquiry

Integrated Processes
Observing
Predicting
Collecting and recording data
Comparing and contrasting
Interpreting data
Relating

Materials
Dependent on student plans

Background Information
Throughout history, people in outdoor occupations such as farming, fishing, or sheepherding were very aware of the weather because it directly affected their work. They looked for patterns—in the sky, in plant and animal life, and in their own bodies—that would help predict the weather. These observations became sayings or proverbs, often given in easy-to-remember verse. Weather proverbs are found in many different cultures, although the ones presented in this book are predominantly from the United States and Europe.

Some proverbs are based on solid science, others have a grain of truth in them (valid at times or in certain locations), and some are false. An example of the latter: Thunder curdles cream or lightning sours milk. As a National Oceanic and Atmospheric Administration (NOAA) publication states, "The trouble with weather proverbs is not so much that they're all wrong, but that they're not all right for all times in all places."[1] This makes proverbs ripe for testing using the scientific process.

Students can make predictions, decide what kind of data need to be collected and how much data is enough to draw a conclusion, and communicate their results. They may need to watch the sky or the behavior of a particular plant or animal as well as the current weather conditions or those which follow. A study of weather proverbs blends together history, language arts, science, and math.

1. National Oceanic and Atmospheric Administration. *The Amateur Weather Forecaster.* Vol. 9, Number 4. October 1979. (NOAA reprint of "Weather Proverbs by R.E. Spencer, formerly of the National Weather Service, first published in the December 27, 1954 issue of the *Weekly Weather and Crop Bulletin.*)

Management
1. Weather proverbs are presented near the beginning of each of the four major sections of *Weather Sense*—temperature, air pressure, wind, and moisture. You are encouraged to use this process and activity page each time you begin a study of a new weather element.

2. This activity will be done over a period of time. Allow at least one day for students to gather weather proverbs from their families (the first time only), another day to choose a proverb and design a plan to test it, a period of time—possibly several weeks—in which to gather data, and then further time to organize and report their results.
3. Each group of students will need to design a plan first in order to know what materials will need to be gathered.

The following is offered for those students ready for more independent work.

Open-ended: Issue the *Challenge* and, without the guidance of leading questions, encourage each student group to devise a plan for testing a proverb.

Procedure
First time
1. Have students ask their parents, grandparents, or family friends about weather sayings they have heard. Record their findings on a class chart that can be on view throughout their weather study.
2. Explain that before weather instruments were invented, people—particularly farmers, shepherds, sailors, and others who worked outdoors—would observe the skies, animals, and plants around them for signs of changing weather. Over time, people developed sayings or proverbs based on their observations.

   Tell students that they will be examining some of these proverbs and then pick one to test for its truthfulness or accuracy.

Each time
1. Give each group one of the proverbs pages—temperature, air pressure, wind, or moisture—or study the list of collected proverbs.
2. Distribute the planning page. Have each group choose a proverb and use the planning page to design the investigation.
3. Gather the necessary materials and instruct students to implement their plans.
4. Allow sufficient time for groups to organize and present their data and conclusions. Encourage them to make a drawing illustrating their proverb.
5. Repeat this activity when another weather element is presented.

Discussion
1. What kinds of jobs are most affected by weather? [construction workers, pilots, farmers, ranchers, fishermen, taxicab drivers, etc.]
2. What was the most difficult part about testing the proverb you chose?

3. How accurate (true) is the proverb you chose? Do you feel you have gathered enough data to be sure of your conclusion? Why or why not?
4. What further questions do you have as a result of your test?

Teacher Resources
Davis, Hubert. *A January Fog Will Freeze a Hog.* Crown Publishers. New York. 1977. (currently out of print but may be found in a library)

Dolan, Edward F. *The Old Farmer's Almanac Book of Weather Lore.* Ivy Books (Ballantine). New York. 1988.

Freier, George D. *Weather Proverbs.* Fisher Books. Tucson, AZ. 1989.

Jones, M. Gail and Glenda Carter. "Weather Folklore: Fact or Fiction?" *Science and Children.* September, 1995. (Gives examples of how specific weather proverbs were tested by students.)

Lee, Albert. *Weather Wisdom.* Doubleday. Garden City, NY. 1976. (out of print)

Lockhart, Gary. *The Weather Companion.* John Wiley & Sons, Inc. New York. 1988.

Sloane, Eric. *Folklore of American Weather.* Duell, Sloan and Pearce. New York. 1963. (currently out of print)

Proverb Proofs

Proverb

Birds sitting on a telephone line, expect rain

Testing Plan

1. What do you predict will happen?
   I think the proverb is true. Birds will sit on telephone lines before it rains.

2. What will you observe?
   whether there are birds or no birds on telephone lines, the weather which follows

3. How often and for what length of time will you do the observations?
   two times a day (morning and afternoon) for three weeks during a rainy time of year

4. What, if anything, needs to be measured?
   no measurements needed

5. What equipment will you need?
   just a notebook and pencil

6. How will you record the results?
   (table, graph, descriptions of observations, conclusions, etc.)

   Make a T-table: Date | Time | Birds on line? | Weather which follows
   11-28-01 | *9:00 am* | *yes or no* | *fair, cloudy, rain, etc.*

   Make a bar graph: When Birds Sat on the Line

   Number of Times

   Fair | Cloudy | Rainy
   Weather Which Followed

   Write conclusions.

Performance Assessment

For older students who have had multiple prior experiences designing and carrying out investigations, this activity might be used as a performance assessment of process skills.

Learning Goals
- Identify the relevant variables to be observed
- Gather sufficient evidence to prove or disprove a proverb
- Organize and label data in a meaningful table and/or graph, diagram, etc.
- Offer a conclusion supported by the data

Evidence of Learning (Rubric)

	Variables	Evidence	Organization	Conclusion
4 Exceeds expectations	Identifies the key variable as well as time, weather, and any other relevant variable	Gathers abundant data, measured and/or anecdotal	Data is well-organized, titled, and labeled in two meaningful ways; work is neat, clear and legible	Thoughtful conclusion supported by data; creative presentation or raises a new question/hypothesis
3 Matches expectations	Identifies the relevant variables, including time and weather	Gathers a sufficient amount of data	Organizes data in at least one meaningful way, legible	States a conclusion supported by data
2 Attempts to meet expectations	Identifies some, but not all, relevant variables or includes an irrelevant variable	Amount of data is a little less than adequate	Data partially organized, labels may be incomplete	Conclusion not fully supported by data, may project opinion or expected conclusion
1 Minimal attempt to meet expectations	Identifies insufficient variables or both relevant and irrelevant variables	Obvious lack of sufficient data	Data not accurately represented, unorganized, and/or incomplete	Conclusion not supported by data or no conclusion offered

* Reprinted with permission from *Principles and Standards for School Mathematics,* 2000 by the National Council of Teachers of Mathematics. All rights reserved.

Proverb Proofs

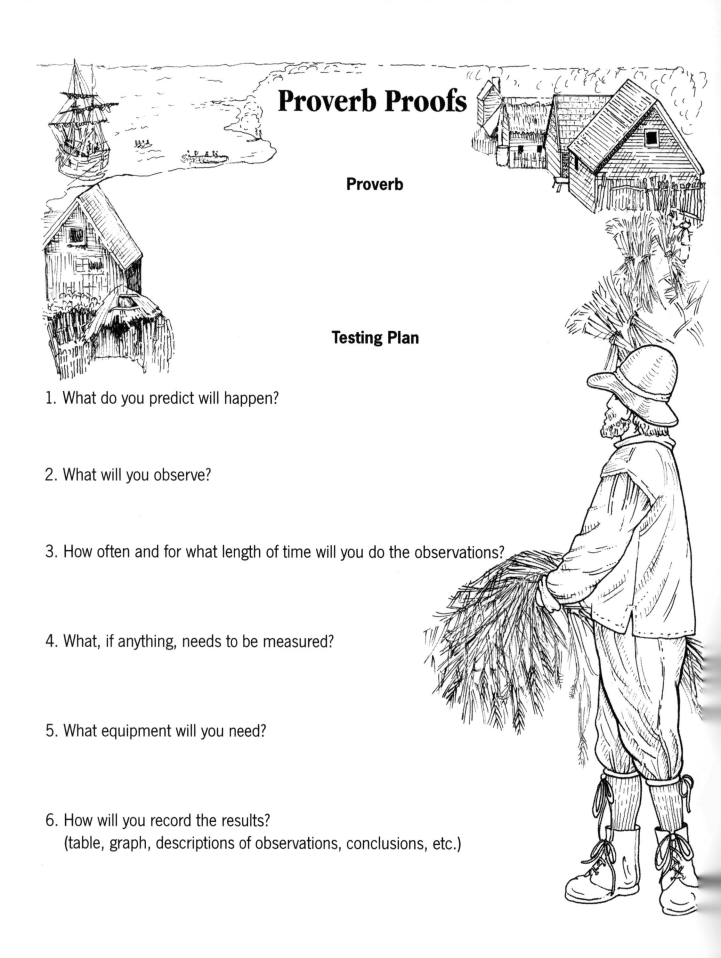

Proverb

Testing Plan

1. What do you predict will happen?

2. What will you observe?

3. How often and for what length of time will you do the observations?

4. What, if anything, needs to be measured?

5. What equipment will you need?

6. How will you record the results?
   (table, graph, descriptions of observations, conclusions, etc.)

Station Model

Topic
Displaying weather data: graphic model

Key Questions
1. How can we show weather data at a glance?
2. How can we use current weather data to forecast the weather?

Focus
Students will learn to construct and interpret a "station model," a concise, graphic display of weather conditions used by meteorologists on surface weather maps. The station model will also be used to forecast weather.

Guiding Documents
Project 2061 Benchmarks
- *Geometric figures, number sequences, graphs, diagrams, sketches, number lines, maps, and stories can be used to represent objects, events, and processes in the real world, although such representations can never be exact in every detail.*
- *Things change in steady, repetitive, or irregular ways—or sometimes in more than one way at the same time. Often the best way to tell which kinds of change are happening is to make a table or graph of measurements.*

NRC Standards
- *Weather changes from day to day and over the seasons. Weather can be described by measurable quantities, such as temperature, wind direction and speed, and precipitation.*
- *Use appropriate tools and techniques to gather, analyze, and interpret data.*

NCTM Standards 2000*
- *Select and apply appropriate standard units and tools to measure length, area, volume, weight, time, temperature, and the size of angles*
- *Collect data using observations, surveys, and experiments*
- *Use representations to model and interpret physical, social, and mathematical phenomena*

Math
Estimation
   area (sky cover)
Measurement
   temperature
   air pressure
   angle, optional for wind speed
   depth (rain gauge)
Graphic model

Science
Earth science
   meteorology

Integrated Processes
Observing
Collecting and recording data
Comparing and contrasting
Interpreting data
Relating
Predicting

Materials
Black and white construction paper (see *Management*)
2-inch to 3-inch squares of white/pastel construction paper or sticky notes (see *Management*)
Black felt-tipped pens
Pushpins

Background Information
A station model is a concise graphic used by meteorologists to show weather conditions for a particular location. The position of each data entry is specified as shown on the *Station Model* page. Though the station model can show a formidable amount of data, only the basic data students will be gathering are incorporated here. Several charts showing the symbols used by meteorologists are also included. There is no designated location for relative humidity on the model.

Data from the following activities should be added to the station model as these weather elements are studied.

Sky cover:	*Sky Cover,* chart included here
Present weather:	chart included here
Temperature:	*Temperature Tally*
Barometric tendency:	*Highs and Lows,* chart included here
Barometric pressure:	*Aneroid Barometer* or *Highs and Lows*
Wind direction:	*Wind Ways,* compass rose
Wind speed:	*Just a Gust?,* chart included here
Precipitation:	*Rain Check*

This activity is both the beginning of the weather unit and the culmination. By the time students have worked their way through the various facets of weather, they will be ready to make more complete records using the table. Based on this information, some limited forecasting for the local area can be done. This lays the foundation for future, more informed forecasting through the examination of weather patterns across the country such as isotherms, isobars, high and low pressure systems, and fronts.

Management

Location

Identify a section of the bulletin board, perhaps by a yarn or paper border, for the station model. Label the model with either your city or school name. Attach data, written on construction paper squares, and symbols with pushpins.

If bulletin board space is not available, a 12" x 18" piece of laminated construction paper can provide the field for the station model. Numerical data can be written on sticky notes and symbols (sky cover and wind) attached with tape or similar means.

Materials

Make one copy of each symbol chart to display near the station model. Add the appropriate chart when a new weather element is introduced. Additional copies of the charts may be made for small groups or individual students, if desired.

Prepare, or have students prepare, the six sky cover symbols (black and white) and the wind symbols (black) from construction paper. The *Templates* page can be used as a guide. Assemble the wind symbols, as needed, with pushpins or tape. To extend their usefulness, consider laminating.

Time

At first, the station model will only show sky cover and present weather. Over time, as the different concepts are studied, temperature, air pressure, wind direction and speed, and precipitation will be added to the model.

Update the station model at a certain time each day or at more frequent intervals. Once started, it takes very little time for students to maintain the station model all year, even after formal weather studies have concluded.

Procedure

Introduction

1. Give students the *Station Model* page and study it together.
2. Present the *Sky Cover* chart, since sky cover is the basis around which the model is built. Take the class outside to an open area. Have students look at the entire visible sky, estimate the percentage that is covered with clouds of any kind, and choose the corresponding sky cover symbol.
3. Introduce the *Present Weather* chart. Explain that these are some of the most common symbols used to describe weather. Curious students can locate additional symbols by searching the Internet.
4. Have a student draw the proper symbol on a sticky note or small piece of paper and position it correctly on the station model. If the weather is fair, no symbol will be displayed.

After "Temperature Tally"

Instruct students to add temperature data to the model, including °C or °F, by writing it on a sticky note or construction paper square.

After "Highs and Lows"

Explain that the balloon barometer can indicate barometric tendency—change in the last three hours. Have students compare their current and previous data to determine whether the air pressure is rising, steady, or falling, then place the correct symbol from the barometric tendency chart on the model. Inform them that this is a key indicator of coming weather.

rising   steady   falling

Optional: Using the non-customary units on the balloon barometer's scale, instruct students to add the barometric pressure on the station model.

After "Aneroid Barometer"

In lieu of the non-customary balloon barometer measurement, have students add the millibars (or inches) measurement of barometric pressure to the station model.

After "Wind Ways"

Display the *Wind Direction and Speed* chart. Consult the compass rose, then model how to show the current wind direction by adding a long black bar (see *Management*) to the sky cover symbol.

After "Just a Gust?"

Based on the data gathered, instruct students to determine the wind speed symbol needed from the chart. Have students pin or tape the appropriate barbs and/or pennants to the long bar on the station model.

After "Rain Check" (see AIMS book *Weather Sense: Moisture*)

Have students record the amount of rain or melted snow on a piece of paper, labeled with millimeters or inches, and add it to the station model.

Forecasting

1. Have students keep a daily record of weather data, individually, in groups, or as a class. Students can devise their own record-keeping method or use the table in this activity. The table includes a place where small, successive versions of the station model can be drawn.
2. Instruct students to study the most current or a series of weather data, looking for a trend or pattern. Pay particular attention to the barometric tendency, wind direction, and cloud types, if clouds have been identified. Ask students to forecast what the weather will be like in a few hours or the next day. Forecasts are more easily made if information is gathered more frequently than once a day.
3. Compare actual weather data with predicted weather. Evaluate what was learned.

Discussion

1. Look at the station model. What does it tell you? [At ____ (time), the sky was ___ (sky cover), the temperature was ___, the wind was coming from the ___ (direction) at ___ (speed), and the barometer was ___ (tendency).]
2. As you study several of the most recent station models, what patterns or trends, if any, do you notice?
3. What kind of weather do you predict we will have later today or tomorrow? (Example: A rainstorm is likely.) On what did you base your prediction? (Students should refer to specific measurements on the station model. Example: The barometer is falling and we know that lower pressure can mean a storm is coming. Also, the wind is coming from the south and, in our area, that usually means rain or snow. Because the temperature is well above freezing, I think we will have rain rather than snow.)
4. Compare weather records from different seasons: How does our weather in fall compare with our weather in winter (or other seasons)?
5. Relate a country-wide weather map and your station model: How does our station model relate to the national picture of weather? (Example: There is a cold front moving in our direction and a low pressure area nearby. That explains why our barometer and the temperature are dropping and the wind is getting stronger. A storm is on the way.)

Extensions

1. Station models can also be used to show weather in other places, using data gathered from newspapers, television weather reports, and the Internet. Encourage each group to choose a city (maybe tied to history studies), locate its weather data, construct a station model, and place the model on a large map. Reduce the size of the station models so they do not obscure the map. You may wish to focus on cities in your state, across the United States, or around the world.
2. Look at surface weather maps which show partial station models on the Internet (see *Weather Websites*).

Station Model

A station model is a special way to display the weather conditions at any given location. Each piece of information belongs in a specific place. A partial station model is sometimes used on surface weather maps.

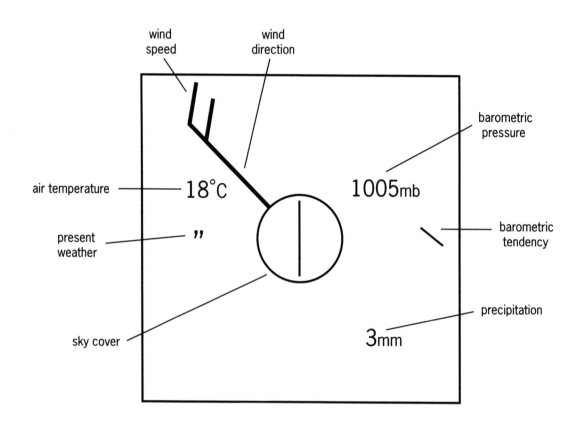

──── Key ────

Sky cover: see *Sky Cover* chart

Present weather: see *Present Weather* chart

Temperature: current air temperature in Celsius or Fahrenheit

Air pressure: air pressure in millibars, millimeters, or inches
Sea level normals are 1013.25 mb, 760 mm, or 29.92 inches.

Barometric tendency:
(change in past 3 hours)

rising   steady   falling

Wind direction and speed: see *Wind Direction and Speed* chart

Precipitation: rain/snow during the last 6 hours in millimeters or hundredths of an inch

Station Model
Templates

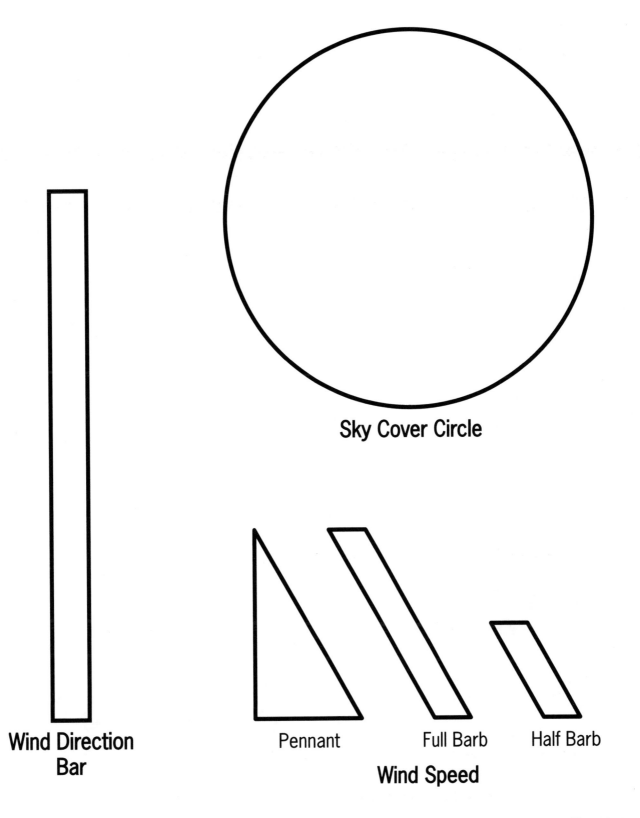

Sky Cover Circle

Wind Direction
Bar

Pennant

Full Barb

Half Barb

Wind Speed

Sky Cover

	Clear	No clouds
	Few	present but < 10%
	Scattered	10 - 50%
	Broken	50 - 90%
	Overcast	more than 90%
	Obscured	**cannot be observed** (possibly fog, haze, blowing snow, smoke, volcanic ash, dust, sand, sea spray, heavy rain, or heavy snow)

Present Weather

Reduced Visibility	Drizzle	Rain	Snow	Other Precipitation	Thunderstorm	Other
smoke	slight	slight	slight	slight rain and snow	slight/moderate	lightning
haze	moderate	moderate	moderate	sleet	heavy	funnel clouds
light fog	heavy	heavy	heavy	slight hail	slight/moderate with rain	
heavy fog	slight freezing (glaze)		slight/moderate drifting	moderate/ heavy hail	slight/moderate with snow	
slight/moderate dust/sandstorm					slight/moderate with hail	
severe dust/sandstorm						

Wind Direction and Speed

Wind Speed
(1 knot = 1.85 km/h or 1.15 mph)

Symbol	Knots	Kilometers per hour	Miles (Statute) per hour
⊚	Calm	Calm	Calm
	1-2	1-4	1-2
	3-7	5-13	3-8
	8-12	14-23	9-14
	13-17	24-32	15-20
	18-22	33-41	21-25
	23-27	42-50	26-31
	28-32	51-60	32-37
	33-37	61-69	38-43
	38-42	70-79	44-49
	43-47	80-87	50-54
	48-52	88-97	55-60
	53-57	98-106	61-66
	58-62	107-115	67-71
	63-67	116-124	72-77
	68-72	125-134	78-83
	73-77	135-143	84-89
	103-107	190-198	119-123

Wind Direction

Use the compass rose to position the bar extending from the sky cover symbol.

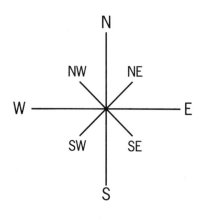

Weather Station Chart

Date/Time	Station Model				
Station Model	○	○	○	○	○
Sky Cover					
Present Weather					
Temperature					
Barometric Tendency					
Barometric Pressure					
Wind Direction and Speed					
Precipitation					

Heat Transfer

The sun's heat energy drives the weather on Earth. The transfer of heat occurs in three different ways: radiation, conduction, and convection.

Solar energy warms the Earth by **radiation**, the process whereby energy travels through space from one location to another. The sun's energy is transported by electromagnetic waves, mostly visible light with the remainder largely infrared radiation. Some of the energy is reflected (about 30%), some is absorbed in the atmosphere (about 20%), and some is absorbed by land and water on the Earth's surface (about 50%). When you feel the warmth of the sun or the warmth of a fire, you are experiencing radiation.

Radiation

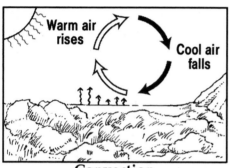
Convection

Convection is the transfer of heat by the movement of a liquid or a gas such as air. As air is warmed at the surface of the Earth, it becomes less dense than surrounding air and rises. As the warm air reaches higher altitudes, it cools, then descends to begin the cycle again. This circulation is called a convection current; its source of energy is often a temperature difference. Hot air rising from the asphalt and water boiling on a stove are other examples of convection at work.

Conduction is the transfer of heat by direct contact, usually through solids. By conduction, heat energy travels along a metal spoon placed in hot soup. Because of conduction, the air in contact with the Earth's surface warms during the day and cools during the night. Air, however, is a poor heat conductor compared to metal.

Conduction

Unequal Heating of the Earth

Everything that absorbs heat energy also radiates heat—the Earth, the clouds, human beings. The balance between incoming solar energy and the energy radiating from the Earth and clouds determines the temperature—the measure of hotness or coldness—of the air and the Earth's surface. Temperature increases when matter absorbs more heat energy than it radiates and decreases when more heat energy is lost than is gained.

There is a nearly perfect balance of heat energy between Earth and the sun. Incoming energy from the sun is relatively equal to the outgoing energy radiating from Earth back into space. Even a slight alteration in this equilibrium can result in the warming or cooling of the Earth and changes in global climate patterns.

While the overall heat energy exchanged between Earth and sun is in balance, this energy is not uniformly absorbed on Earth due to 1) the Earth's daily rotation on its axis, 2) the tilt of the Earth as it revolves around the sun, 3) variations in how land and water masses absorb and lose heat energy, and 4) cloud cover. *It is the unequal heating of the Earth's atmosphere, oceans and land masses that puts the atmosphere in motion, producing our weather; the atmosphere is seeking a state of equilibrium.*

Earth's Rotation

The Earth's daily rotation on its axis causes the night and day cycle. The side of the Earth facing the sun is heated while the dark side cools. *Time of day* affects the temperature. The lowest temperature commonly occurs near sunrise, after several hours of cooling darkness. During midday, the sun's most direct, intense rays are emitting heat energy. The effects of this heating take time to accumulate (heat lag), so the highest temperature is often recorded during the late afternoon hours.

Earth's Revolution with a Tilted Axis

The tilt of the Earth's axis as it makes its yearly revolution around the sun affects temperature in two ways. For most locations other than the Equatorial region, the *length of day* changes throughout the year. One reason temperatures in the Northern Hemisphere are higher in the summer is because the longer daylight hours permit more solar energy to be absorbed. The shorter daylight hours of winter are cooler, partly because there are fewer hours of exposure to solar energy. If the Earth were *not* tilted, the length of day would remain the same—12 hours—all year long throughout the world.

The Earth's 23.5° tilt also causes the *sun's elevation above the horizon* to change throughout the year. The higher the sun appears in the sky, the more directly (and more intensely) its rays strike the Earth. In the Northern Hemisphere, the sun's highest elevation for a given latitude is reached at solar noon on summer solstice. At 37°N, for example, the sun's highest position in summer is 76° above the horizon while its highest winter position is 26° above the horizon. Regions under the sun's direct (perpendicular or near perpendicular) rays receive more solar energy than regions under more indirect rays.

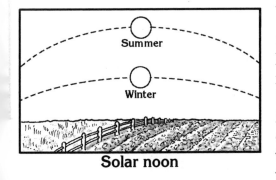

Solar noon

The Earth's tilt and revolution around the sun cause five heat zones on Earth: the Tropical Zone which receives the sun's most direct rays, the two Temperate Zones which receive sunshine all year but in varying amounts, and the two Polar Zones which not only receive the sun's most indirect rays but plunge into darkness for part of the year.

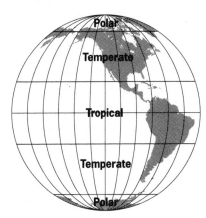

Land and Water

Land and water masses absorb heat differently because of their *physical properties*. Land is generally dark, opaque, and relatively motionless. Since soil is not transparent, it absorbs the sun's rays only at its surface. Darker surfaces absorb more heat energy than lighter surfaces. A grassy field, for example, reflects only 10% to 30% of heat energy back into space while snow reflects 75% to 95%.

Water, on the other hand, is transparent and in constant motion. Sunlight can pass into it and be distributed over a greater depth by the movement of the water. Water holds heat a long time, releasing it very slowly into the atmosphere. This causes water to have a more uniform, moderate temperature whereas land is quickly cooled by the loss of heat at its surface.

As a result, land areas generally have greater temperature extremes than ocean areas during the night/day cycle. Seasonal temperatures follow the same pattern: land climates tend to be warmer in summer and cooler in winter than ocean climates at the same latitude.

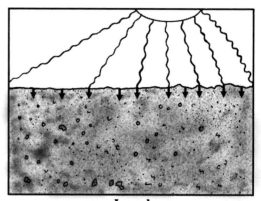

Land

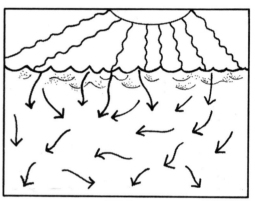

Water

Cloud Cover

The *amount of cloud cover* partially determines how much heat energy enters and leaves the Earth. A clear sky allows heat energy to move freely in both directions. Thin clouds reflect 30% to 50%. But if the Earth has a thick blanket of clouds, as much as 95% of the solar energy may be reflected back toward the sun, meaning very few solar rays penetrate the Earth. For the same reason, the heat energy previously absorbed by the Earth is trapped, with very little radiating back into space.

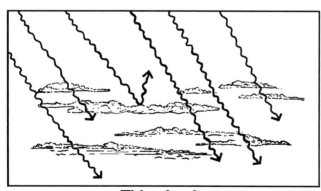

Thin clouds

Thick clouds

Thermometers and Scales

The temperature of the air is measured with thermometers. Mercury and alcohol are most often used in thermometers because they respond easily to hot and cold. As temperatures rise, the liquid expands and climbs up the tube. As temperatures fall, the liquid contracts and drops.

Before 1600, people described temperature by how it felt to them: cold, comfortable, warm, or hot. There were no thermometers. Galileo made an air thermometer in 1593 but it was fragile, hard to move, and not very accurate.

In order for scientists in different locations to compare temperatures, a reliable scale of measurement was needed. Scientists tried to find a liquid that would expand and contract evenly. They experimented with everything from melted butter to animal blood. In 1714, a physicist named Daniel Fahrenheit found that mercury worked well. The scale he created made no more sense than the previous ones, but because of its accuracy, it became the one used for many years.

Gabriel Daniel Fahrenheit
1686 (Poland)—1736 (Netherlands)

Daniel Fahrenheit was born to a wealthy merchant family in what is now Gdansk, Poland. After the sudden death of his parents in 1701, Daniel moved to Amsterdam where he became a maker of scientific instruments.

His most important achievement was the invention of the first accurate thermometer. He developed a temperature scale based on the movement of mercury, a liquid metal that expands and contracts with temperature changes but does not evaporate. It is called the Fahrenheit scale.

Imagine starting with a thin tube containing mercury and no markings. How would you decide where to put the lines and numbers? Fahrenheit marked four points to make his scale.

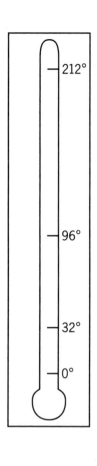

1st: He wanted a scale that would avoid negative numbers below freezing. On a very cold day, he mixed salt with ice water to lower the temperature. This was thought to be the coldest temperature possible. Fahrenheit labeled the level of mercury in the tube 0°.

2nd: Fahrenheit's second point was normal human body temperature which he mistakenly labeled at 96°. This was later corrected to 98.6°.

3rd: Dividing the space between 0 and 96 into 96 equal parts, he found that water freezes at 32°.

4th: Continuing up his scale, he discovered that water boils at 212°.

Anders Celsius

1701 (Uppsala, Sweden)—1744 (Uppsala, Sweden)

Anders Celsius was born into a family of scientists and mathematicians. He was an astronomy professor, but is best known for developing a decimal-based thermometer scale in 1742. He reasoned that there should only be two fixed points, the freezing point of water which he labeled 100° and the boiling point of water which he labeled 0°. The scale was soon reversed, putting the freezing temperature at 0° and the boiling temperature at 100°–the form we use today. It was most often called the "Swedish thermometer" or the centigrade scale (cent=100, grade=degree or step) until the mid-1900s when scientists generally agreed to rename it the Celsius scale. Today, most of the civilized world and scientists everywhere use the Celsius scale.

Comparing Scales

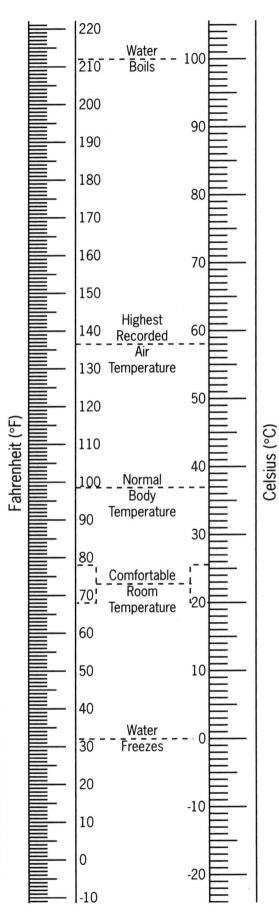

How many degrees from freezing to boiling?

Celsius scale:

Fahrenheit scale:

The important thing to remember is that the same things happen at the same temperatures, no matter what scale is used. Water always boils at the same temperature, whether the scale reads 100°C or 212°F.

Degrees Celsius

Thirty is hot.

Twenty is nice.

Ten is cool.

Zero is ice.

—Anonymous

Temperature Proverbs

Proverbs are short, common-sense sayings based on people's observations. Which ones do you think are accurate predictors of weather? Design an investigation to test one of the proverbs.

Critters

When ladybugs swarm,
    expect a day that's warm.

If spiders are many
    and spinning their webs,
    the weather is fair.

The wider the black bands on
    a woolly bear caterpillar,
    the colder the winter will be.

A cricket's chirp
    tells the temperature.

When ants travel in a straight line,
    expect rain;
When they scatter,
    expect fair weather.

Birds

When birds huddle at the top of a chimney,
It is a sign of cold weather.

Birds sitting on a telephone line, expect rain.

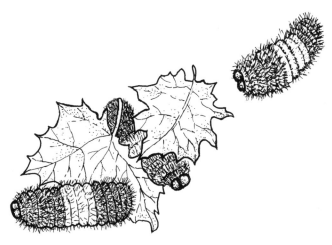

This and That

Dew on the grass,
No rain will pass.

Cold is the night,
When the stars shine bright.

The chills are on from near and far
In all the months that have an R.

Thunder in spring
Cold will bring.

Flowers

Open crocus, warm weather;
Closed crocus, cold weather.

Tulips open their blossoms
    when the temperature rises,
they close again when the
    temperature falls.

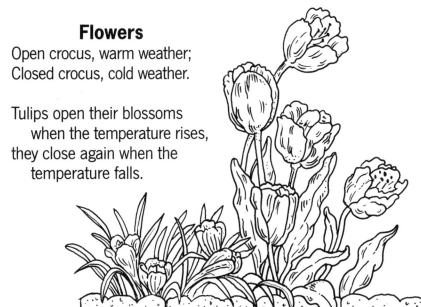

Temperature Proverbs

Teacher Notes

"The trouble with weather proverbs is not so much that they're all wrong, but that they're not all right for all times in all places."

NOAA reprint of "Weather Proverbs" by R.E. Spencer (1979)

Flowers

Open crocus, warm weather;
Closed crocus, cold weather.

Tulips open their blossoms
*   when the temperature rises,*
they close again when the
*   temperature falls.*

Birds

When birds huddle at the top
*   of a chimney,*
It is a sign of cold weather.

Birds sitting on a telephone line,
*   expect rain.*

Critters

When ladybugs swarm,
*   expect a day that's warm.*

If spiders are many
*   and spinning their webs,*
*   the weather is fair.*

The wider the black bands on
*   a woolly bear caterpillar,*
*   the colder the winter will be.*

A cricket's chirp
*   tells the temperature.*

When ants travel in a straight line,
*   expect rain;*
When they scatter,
*   expect fair weather.*

This and That

Dew on the grass,
*   no rain will pass.*

Cold is the night,
When the stars shine bright.

The chills are on from near and far
In all the months that have an R.

Thunder in spring
Cold will bring.

Comments

Crocuses and tulips are temperature-sensitive. Botanists say you can tell the temperature to the nearest half degree by observing how far a crocus has opened. Pick a wide-open tulip on a warm spring day, place it in the refrigerator, and it will close into a tight bud. When removed, it opens again.

Lower air pressure—a feature of a front bringing cooler temperatures and the likelihood of rain—makes it more difficult for birds to fly. At such times, several species tend to perch.

No scientific basis.

Moisture causes spider webs to contract, destroying them. Long filaments are only seen when the weather is dry.

Some have found this to be a reliable predictor, others have not.

Crickets are cold-blooded so they reflect the temperature of their surroundings. To find °F, count the number of chirps in 14 seconds, then add 40.

Doubtful. No scientific basis.

Dew forms when the air is relatively dry and the skies are clear, conditions of a high-pressure, fair-weather system. The surface on which it forms must be colder than the dew-point temperature.

The air cools more on clear nights since heat energy readily escapes into space. In contrast, clouds act like a blanket, trapping heat energy radiating from Earth.

May or may not be true for your location.

Thunder is not a predictor of weather.

Playground FEVER

Topic
Temperatures in a microclimate

Key Question
How do our playground temperatures compare?

Focus
Based on temperature data collected from different areas of the schoolyard, students will discover that location affects temperature. They should begin to hypothesize about variables which might cause temperature differences.

Guiding Documents
Project 2061 Benchmarks
- *Measuring instruments can be used to gather accurate information for making scientific comparisons of objects and events and for designing and constructing things that will work properly.*
- *Offer reasons for their findings and consider reasons suggested by others.*

NRC Standards
- *Plan and conduct a simple investigation.*
- *Employ simple equipment and tools to gather data and extend the senses.*
- *Use data to construct a reasonable explanation.*

NCTM Standards 2000*
- *Select and apply appropriate standard units and tools to measure length, area, volume, weight, time, temperature, and the size of angles*
- *Collect data using observations, surveys, and experiments*

Math
Measurement
  temperature

Science
Earth science
  meteorology
Physical science
  heat energy

Integrated Processes
Observing
Collecting and recording data
Comparing and contrasting
Interpreting data
Hypothesizing

Materials
6 or more thermometers
1 meter stick or ruler per thermometer, optional
Map of your school

Background Information
This open-ended activity is mostly about raising questions, about drawing students into a state of wondering, rather than about finding answers. Answers will come later, as further investigations are done. Variables are purposely not controlled so that students will begin to question and identify what some of those variables are.

The one conclusion that should be reached is that even a microclimate, a small area such as a schoolyard, can have varying temperatures. Students may know this intuitively from their own experiences outdoors, but probably have not given it much conscious thought nor gathered supporting scientific evidence. As students ponder why the outdoor temperatures vary and then form hypotheses, they may also begin to question which location meteorologists would use for an official temperature reading.

Management
1. Make copies of your school map, one for each group or one per student. It will be used to record temperatures at each location. You may also wish to make a map transparency or enlarged map for use during class discussions.
2. To make valid comparisons, thermometers with matching readings are preferred. However, differing thermometers may be made equivalent by computation. Choose a baseline thermometer and determine by how much the others differ. Tape the amount to be added or subtracted (+1, -2, etc.) to these thermometers.

3. For measurements to be precise, a person must identify the kind of thermometer scale (Celsius or Fahrenheit), recognize the increments on the scale, wait for the thermometer liquid to stop moving, bring eyes level or perpendicular to the scale, and read carefully. (See the activity, *A Matter of Degrees.*)

4. Take care not to touch the thermometer bulb since body heat can change the temperature. If each thermometer is attached to a meter stick or ruler, the stick can be gripped rather than the thermometer.

5. Divide the class into a minimum of six groups, each of which will choose a different location from which to collect data. All data should be gathered at the same time.

6. This activity is best done on a warm, sunny day with little wind, conditions in which the sun's radiation magnifies the effects of unequal heating.

Procedure

1. Present the following scenario or a similar one applicable to your class: "On a very warm day, you decide to play basketball during recess. When you need a place to cool off while still outside, where would you go?" [under a tree, etc.] Ask, "What might make this place cooler than the basketball court?" [It is out of the sun.] "I wonder, how do our playground temperatures compare?" Have students make oral predictions, including how big or small the temperature range will be.

2. Give students the activity page and map. Guide groups—to ensure variety—as they determine where the thermometers should be placed (near the flag pole, in the parking lot, on the basketball court, under a tree, next to a classroom, in a flower bed, etc.)

3. Review procedures for taking precise measurements (see *Management 3*) and distribute the thermometers.

4. Instruct each group to place a thermometer at the chosen location. While waiting for the thermometer to register the temperature, a group recorder or each group member should write a description of the location in as much detail as possible. A few prompts are given.

5. After the temperature and time have been recorded, return to the classroom. Have groups report data, with each student recording the temperatures and brief, descriptive words at the appropriate location on his or her map.

6. Study and discuss observations together, then have students respond to the questions at the bottom of the page.

7. Encourage students to develop hypotheses based on their initial findings. Write the hypotheses on chart paper, the chalkboard, or a transparency so they can be referred to as further investigations are completed.

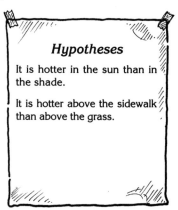

Hypotheses

It is hotter in the sun than in the shade.

It is hotter above the sidewalk than above the grass.

Discussion

1. What is the temperature at our school? (This question should raise puzzled expressions since it is unlikely there is one uniform temperature. Students should generalize that temperature varies with the location. As to which should be reported as the school's temperature, leave that to be answered after doing *On Location* and/or *Extension 1*.)

2. What was the range of temperatures in our schoolyard? (Find the difference between the highest and lowest recorded temperatures.)

3. Where in our schoolyard might the temperature be even warmer than the highest temperature we recorded? Where might it be even cooler than the lowest temperature we recorded? (To test these guesses, place one thermometer at the location of the previous highest temperature and another at the location predicted to surpass it. Do the same for the cool temperatures.)

4. Compare two locations: Why do you think it was warmer here than over there? Repeat with another pair of locations. (Record the possible variables that are mentioned. Ask students what variables could be put together in a group. Guide students in grouping variables by type and giving each type a name. For example, items like grass, concrete, asphalt, dirt, etc., could be in a group called "surfaces.")

5. What are you wondering?

6. What hypothesis would you like to test? Design an investigation to test it and follow your plan (see *On Location*).

Extensions

1. Ask, "If our school has more than one temperature, how about our town?" [It will have different temperatures in different places, too.] "The news only reports one high temperature for our town, so where is this temperature reading taken? How was this particular spot chosen?" Challenge students to research the answers. One possible resource is the nearest National Weather Service station.

2. If this activity is done in warm, sunny weather as suggested, repeat it on a cool, sunny day or a warm, cloudy day and compare the results. How will the temperature range compare in different kinds of weather? ...with different amounts of cloud cover?

Home Link

Put several thermometers in a resealable plastic bag and have students take turns doing thermometer readings at various locations outside or inside their houses.

* Reprinted with permission from *Principles and Standards for School Mathematics*, 2000 by the National Council of Teachers of Mathematics. All rights reserved.

Connections

The sun is the driving force of weather. The amount of solar energy that interacts with the Earth and its atmosphere depends primarily on the angle at which the sun's rays strike the Earth, the degree to which Earth's materials absorb and emit the heat energy, and the amount of cloud cover. In *Playground Fever* we found that the temperature due to the sun's heat energy varies, even within a small area—the schoolyard. Since the investigation was performed within a short time period, the angle of the sun and amount of cloud cover probably did not change. So a hypothesis could be made that the unequal heating was due to the extent that materials on the Earth absorbed and emitted heat energy. Let's test that hypothesis in the next activity, *On Location*. In it we will explore the variables on the surface of the Earth which contribute to unequal heating.

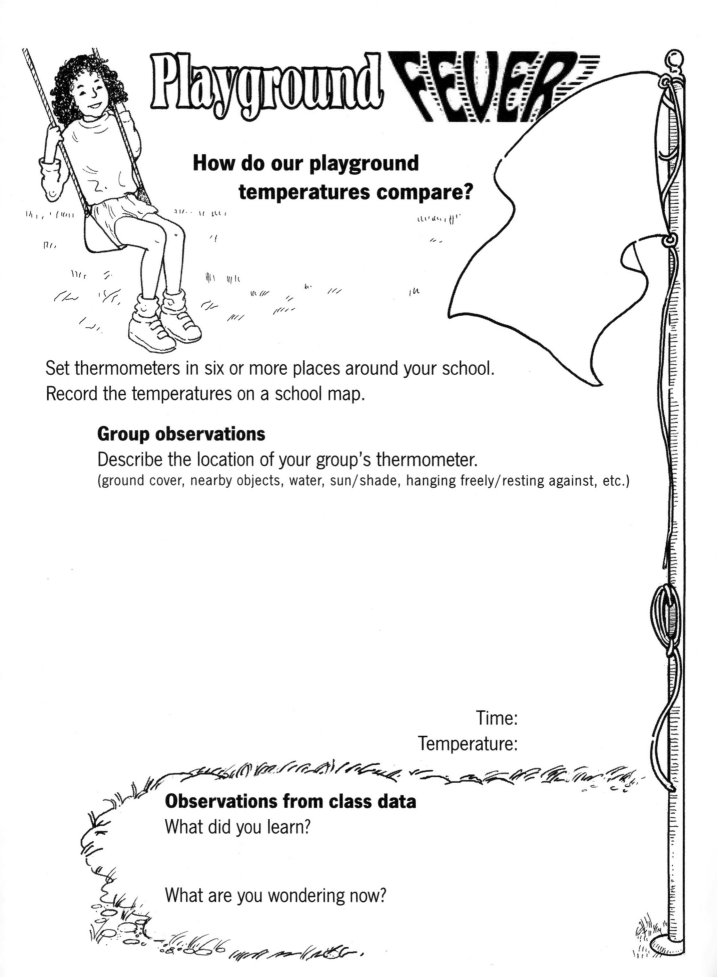

Playground FEVER

How do our playground temperatures compare?

Set thermometers in six or more places around your school.
Record the temperatures on a school map.

Group observations
Describe the location of your group's thermometer.
(ground cover, nearby objects, water, sun/shade, hanging freely/resting against, etc.)

Time:
Temperature:

Observations from class data
What did you learn?

What are you wondering now?

ON LOCATION

Topic
Temperature: location variables

Key Question
How does location affect temperature?

Focus
Students will explore how temperatures are influenced by variables such as exposure to the sun, kind of surface, and height above the surface. This information will be linked to the standards used by meteorologists to take temperatures.

Guiding Documents
Project 2061 Benchmarks
- *Measuring instruments can be used to gather accurate information for making scientific comparisons of objects and events and for designing and constructing things that will work properly.*
- *Some materials conduct heat much better than others. Poor conductors can reduce heat loss.*

NRC Standards
- *The sun provides the light and heat necessary to maintain the temperature of the earth.*
- *Employ simple equipment and tools to gather data and extend the senses.*

NCTM Standards 2000*
- *Select and apply appropriate standard units and tools to measure length, area, volume, weight, time, temperature, and the size of angles*
- *Collect data using observations, surveys, and experiments*
- *Represent data using tables and graphs such as line plots, bar graphs, and line graphs*

Math
Measurement
    temperature
    length
Ordering
Graphing
    bar

Science
Earth science
    meteorology
Physical science
    heat energy

Stevenson screen

Integrated Processes
Observing
Predicting
Controlling variables
Collecting and recording data
Comparing and contrasting
Interpreting data

Materials
Thermometers
Meter sticks for thermometers
Tape

Background Information
Temperature at a particular location and time is affected by several variables, among them exposure to the sun, the kind of surface, and the distance from the ground or structures. These variables can cause a relatively small area, such as a schoolyard (*Playground Fever*), to have a range of temperatures rather than one uniform temperature. To measure the temperature of the *air*, which is what is reported in weather data, budding meteorologists need to understand the effects of these variables and how to control them when positioning the thermometer.

Sun exposure
Two friends visit outdoors on a cool day. After the goose bumps set in, they move to a spot in the sun and feel warmer. Is the temperature of the air warmer in that spot? Not necessarily. It is the direct radiation from the sun that warms them.

A thermometer exposed directly to the sun measures more than just the air temperature; it receives and registers the sun's radiant energy as well. And, the fewer the clouds and the more direct the angle of the sun's rays, the greater the amount of radiant energy that reaches Earth. To avoid measuring radiant energy, the thermometer should be shielded from the sun with objects such as a piece of paper, your body, a tree, or protective housing.

National Weather Service meteorologists place the thermometer in a Stevenson screen, a white, wooden, ventilated box with the instruments and door facing north. This box shields the thermometer from direct sun but allows breezes to flow through it. The white paint reflects heat energy better than darker colors. Wood is used because it is a poor conductor of heat energy. The instruments face north because that direction receives the least direct sunlight in the Northern Hemisphere. In the Southern Hemisphere, a southern orientation receives the least direct sunlight.

Kind of surface

On a hot summer day, would a barefoot person feel more comfortable walking across an asphalt road or grass in the yard? Most of us have experienced the burning sensation of the scorching asphalt and would much prefer the coolness of grass.

On average, about half of the solar energy reaching Earth is absorbed while the other half is reflected back into space. How much is absorbed depends on the composition and color of the surface. Some materials, like asphalt, are better conductors than others. Then, too, dark colors absorb more heat energy than light colors.

The table[1] shows the typical amount of solar radiation reflected (albedo) by various surfaces. What is not reflected is absorbed or transmitted. So new snow is absorbing only about 10% of the radiation whereas asphalt is absorbing more than 90%.

Surface	Albedo
New snow	90%
Old snow	50%
Average cloud cover	50%
Light sand	40%
Light soil	25%
Concrete	25%
Green crops	20%
Green forests	15%
Dark soil	10%
Asphalt	8%
Water	8%[2]

Meterologists prefer to measure air temperature above a grassy surface. In the absence of grass, level ground typical of the surrounding area is chosen, though close proximity to paved or concrete surfaces should be avoided.

Distance from ground or structures

Matter that absorbs heat energy also emits heat energy. If a thermometer is placed on or very close to a surface, whether the ground or a building, heat energy from that surface will be conducted to the thermometer; it will register more than just the air temperature. Temperatures on sunny days are usually warmer close to the ground; at night, however, the ground temperature may be cooler than the air temperature since land loses heat quickly. So that heat energy emitted from the surface is not reflected in air temperature readings, the Stevenson screen is positioned 1.5 meters (about 5 feet) above the ground and away from structures.

1. Eagleman, Joe E. *Meteorology: The Atmosphere in Action.* Wadsworth Publishing Company. Belmont, CA. 1985.
2. The albedo for water varies greatly with the angle of the sun's rays. Near sunset, when the rays are very indirect, most of the radiation is reflected.

Management

1. To make valid comparisons, thermometers with matching readings are preferred. However, differing thermometers may be made equivalent by computation. Choose a baseline thermometer and determine by how much the others differ. Tape the amount to be added or subtracted (+1, -2, etc.) to these thermometers.

2. For valid measurements, make sure the thermometer is shaded. For preciseness, identify the scale and scale increments, wait for the thermometer liquid to stop moving, bring the eyes perpendicular to the scale, and read carefully. (See the activity, *A Matter of Degrees.*)

3. Tape the thermometers to meter sticks. They provide a built-in measure and make it easier for students to keep their hands away from the thermometer bulbs, which can be affected by body heat.

4. For optimum temperature contrasts, schedule this investigation when the most radiant heat reaches the Earth, namely when the sun's rays are more direct (hours near solar noon), the days are longer (late spring, summer, or early fall), and there are few or no clouds in the sky.

5. There are several options for implementing this activity.

Open-ended: Students ready for more independent work should follow up their hypotheses from *Playground Fever* by designing, on their own paper, a scientific test for one of the variables (sun exposure, surface, height, etc.) The *Key Question* can also be given: "How does location affect temperature?"

Guided planning: Ask the *Key Question:* "How does location affect temperature?" Have students identify variables they want to explore, based on the *Playground Fever* investigation. On a transparency or chart paper, list questions such as these to help students plan on their own paper:
   What variable are you testing?
   What kinds of locations does this include?
   How are you going to control other variables?
   When and how often will temperature readings be taken?
   How will the results be recorded?
   What did you discover?

More structured: Choose *Option A* in which students focus on variables of their own choosing, one at a time, or *Option B* in which students briefly test three specific variables.

6. If students are doing more in-depth work *(Option A),* plan on testing one variable each day. *Option B* may require one day for testing and another for examining data and writing conclusions.

7. For *Option A,* one page will be needed for each variable tested.

Procedure

Option A

1. Ask, "Does it make a difference where we put the thermometer to take the air temperature outdoors?" (Encourage responses.) "We are going to test how location affects temperature. What kind of variables do you think we might test?" (If at all possible, base the investigation on their responses but somewhere in the mix *sun exposure* (sun, shade), *surfaces* (grass, concrete, sand, asphalt, dirt, etc.), and *height* (0 meters, 1 meter) should be addressed. Proximity to buildings (another distance variable), color, and the presence of water are other possibilities.)

2. Give students the *Option A* activity page. Have them record the variable to be tested and those which will be controlled. Students should also identify **how** they will be controlled.

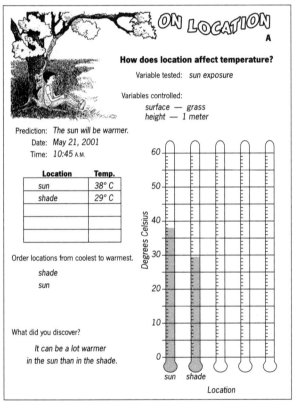

3. Have students predict which location will be warmest.

4. Take the class outside to the appropriate locations. Have students position the thermometers, wait for them to equilibrate, read the temperatures, and record them. Groups of students can each take their own measurements.

5. Back inside, instruct students to rank the locations based on actual data, complete the bar graph, and write their conclusions. Share data between groups.

6. Repeat steps 2-5 for each variable, using a separate page for each. Students should explore a minimum of three variables—sun exposure, surface, and height—in order to understand the standards used by meteorologists for taking air temperature.

 Journal Prompt: What combination of locations would best register just air temperature? Why?

Option B

1. Ask the *Key Question:* "How does location affect temperature?" (Students should reflect on their experience in *Playground Fever*, identifying some of the possible variables. Guide the discussion so that it includes *sun exposure* (sun, shade), *surface* (grass, concrete, sand, asphalt, dirt, etc.), and *height* (0 meters, 1 meter).

2. Distribute the *Option B* page and draw attention to the first variable to be tested: sun exposure. Discuss together over what surface and at what height to conduct the test. A one-meter height is strongly encouraged to counter any effects from the surface.

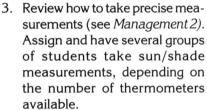

3. Review how to take precise measurements (see *Management 2*). Assign and have several groups of students take sun/shade measurements, depending on the number of thermometers available.

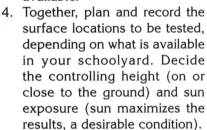

4. Together, plan and record the surface locations to be tested, depending on what is available in your schoolyard. Decide the controlling height (on or close to the ground) and sun exposure (sun maximizes the results, a desirable condition).

5. After repositioning the thermometers on the meter sticks, have student groups measure the temperatures and order the surfaces from cool to warm.

6. Discuss, as a class, the variables to control when testing height. Decide the controlling surface (the surface can vary from group to group) and sun exposure. Again, the sun will yield more variation than shade.

7. Instruct students to tape two thermometers in identical positions, but at opposite ends of the same meter stick, as both readings can be taken at the same time.

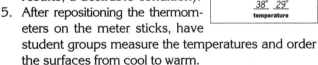

8. After the height measurements are gathered and recorded, have students examine the data.

 Journal prompt: What combination of locations would best register just air temperature? Why?

Discussion

1. What surprised you about the results?
2. How does your group's data compare to others?
3. What combination of variables would give the coolest reading? ...the warmest reading?
4. What standards do you think meteorologists *might* use to take the air temperature? Why? (Encourage students to voice their opinions, but do not expect them to fully determine the standards from their data. At some point, introduce the standards mentioned in *Background Information*.)
5. An announcer of a major championship tennis match, such as the French or U.S. Open, says the temperature is 92°F but on the court it is 101°F. What do you think makes it hotter on the tennis court? [exposure to the sun, the clay or concrete surface, the enclosed space of center court which blocks breezes, the combined heat radiating from all the spectators, etc.]

Extensions

1. Introduce the time variable by doing sun/shade temperature measurements every hour or two throughout the school day. How does the difference between the sun and shade measurements change? [Unless clouds interfere, the difference should increase from morning (more indirect rays) to solar noon (most direct rays) and then decrease toward sunset.]

Time	Location	Temp.
	sun	
	shade	
	sun	
	shade	
	sun	
	shade	

2. To explore how different colors absorb heat energy, do the activity *Hot Pockets*, found in *AIMS®*, Volume XIII, Number 2.

* Reprinted with permission from *Principles and Standards for School Mathematics,* 2000 by the National Council of Teachers of Mathematics. All rights reserved.

Connections

The sun is the source of the Earth's heat energy, but all locations do not heat equally. It is this unequal heating that causes weather. We have found that shady spots are cooler than those exposed to the sun's radiation. Some surfaces, such as asphalt, absorb and radiate more heat energy and, through conduction, raise the temperature of the air close to that surface.

The heat energy investigation just completed relates to the scientific process, too; when meteorologists take measurements, they isolate one variable. To measure the temperature of the air alone, the thermometer is shielded from sun exposure and the effects of varying surfaces by placing it in the shade or a protected, ventilated box 1.5 meters above a grassy surface.

This knowledge of variables will be applied in the next activity, *Temperature Tally*, as we choose an appropriate location for an informal weather station.

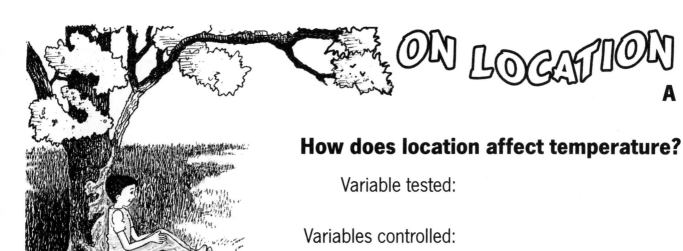

How does location affect temperature?

Variable tested:

Variables controlled:

Prediction:

Date:

Time:

Location	Temp.

Order locations from coolest to warmest.

What did you discover?

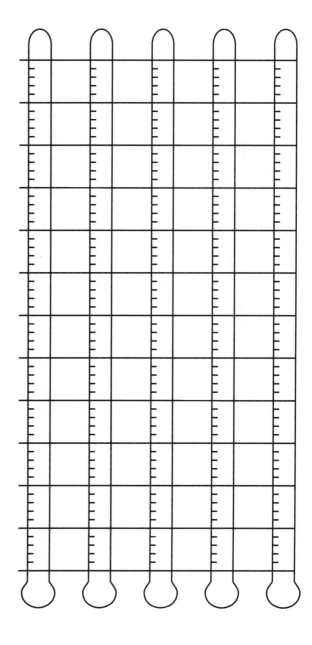

ON LOCATION
B

How does location affect temperature?

Sun exposure	Surface	Height
Variables controlled	Variables controlled	Variables controlled

Degrees

sun | shade

_____ _____
temperature

Location	Temp.
concrete	
grass	

Order from cool to warm.

_____

_____

_____

_____

_____

Degrees

0 m | 1 m

_____ _____
temperature

Temperature

Essential Question

How does location affect temperature?

Learning Goals

- Observe and gather evidence that temperature varies with location, both locally and globally.

  Locally:
  - Explore how local variables—sun exposure, surface, distance from, etc.— affect temperature.
  - Identify possible local weather station sites where these variables will be controlled.

  Globally:
  - Investigate differences in the way land and water absorb and emit the sun's heat energy, contributing to unequal heating.
  - Gather and plot continental temperature data to discover unequal heating patterns related to latitude.

Local Temperature Assessment

Activity

Make copies of a school map to give to each student. Take the class outside and have each student observe and mark two or three places on the map which would be appropriate for taking the air temperature in their schoolyard. Ask students to defend their choices based on the investigations they have done.

Evidence of Learning

Students should acknowledge that temperatures vary with location and that certain variables need to be controlled in order to measure air temperature—and only air temperature. Places chosen should be in the shade, away from buildings, and at least one meter above the ground. A grassy surface is preferable but, in its absence, a level surface typical of the surroundings may be used. Avoid paved or concrete surfaces since they emit a significant amount of heat energy.

Shade is necessary to shield the thermometer from the sun's radiation. Keeping a distance from buildings and ground surfaces minimizes the effects of heat energy being conducted from these sources.

Graphing Thermometer

Materials
Light-colored very stiff railroad board, approx. 44" x 14"
Adding machine paper roll, 2¼" wide
12" pipe cleaner
Sturdy rubber band that stretches to 14"
Permanent ink pen
Tape
Craft knife

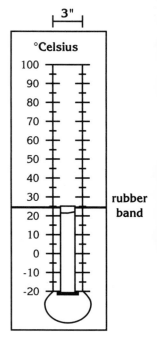

Construction
1. Choose the thermometer scale (Celsius or Fahrenheit) and the increments (1° or 2°), considering the kind of thermometers your students will be using and your goals for the class. Cut out the chosen scale below and mark the railroad board. Allow room at the bottom to draw a thermometer bulb.
2. Optional: Label the following common temperatures.

	°C	°F
Water boils	100	212
Normal body temperature	37	98.6
Room temperature	20-26	68-78
Water freezes	0	32

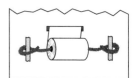

Back of thermometer

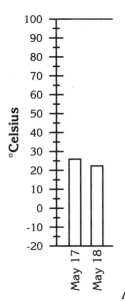

Bar graph

3. Cut a slit the width of the thermometer, ¼ inch below the lowest scale mark.
4. Thread a pipe cleaner through the paper roll. With tape, attach each end of the pipe cleaner to the back of the thermometer just below the slit.
5. Thread the paper through the slit to the front of the thermometer. Make sure it can be pulled easily. Slide a large rubber band over the width of the board.
6. To show the temperature, bring the rubber band to the appropriate level, pull the paper up, and fold a small amount over the rubber band.
7. To make the bar graph, cut the paper band from the bottom scale line to the fold at the rubber band. Display on a wall, adding more bands as new temperature readings are taken. Use the graph to identify and discuss temperature patterns.

A Celsius scale with twelve 10° sections (-20° to 100°) will be about 76 cm (30 in) long

Celsius: 1° scale

A Fahrenheit scale with twenty-one 10° sections (0° to 212°) will be about 79 cm (31 in) long

Fahrenheit: 1° scale

Temperature Tally

Topic
Weather station: air temperature

Key Question
How does the temperature change over time?

Focus
Students will take temperature readings at regular intervals and graph the data, making a visual transition from bar graph to broken-line graph. In an extension, students will compare their own readings to official temperature data gathered via radio, television, or computer.

Guiding Documents
Project 2061 Benchmarks
- *Things change in steady, repetitive, or irregular ways—or sometimes in more than one way at the same time. Often the best way to tell which kinds of change are happening is to make a table or graph of measurements.*
- *Recognize when comparisons might not be fair because some conditions are not kept the same.*

NRC Standard
- *Weather changes from day to day and over the seasons. Weather can be described by measurable quantities, such as temperature, wind direction and speed, and precipitation.*

NCTM Standards 2000*
- *Select and apply appropriate standard units and tools to measure length, area, volume, weight, time, temperature, and the size of angles*
- *Collect data using observations, surveys, and experiments*

Math
Measurement
    temperature
Graphing
    bar and line

Science
Earth science
    meteorology

Technology
Radio, television, or computer

Integrated Processes
Observing
Identifying and controlling variables
Collecting and recording data
Comparing and contrasting
Inferring

Materials
For each group:
    thermometer
    stick or rod, 1 to 1.5 meters tall
    6-8 cm piece of tape

For Extension, access to one of the following:
    NOAA Weather Radio
    television weather information
    Internet

Background Information
The Earth is warmed by energy from the sun. The sun's surface temperature is about 6000°C (11,000°F) while the Earth's surface temperature generally ranges from -51°C to +49°C (-60°F to +120°F). The Earth intercepts only about one two-billionths of the energy the sun radiates.[1] About 50% of this solar energy is absorbed in the ground and oceans, about 20% is absorbed in the atmosphere, and about 30% is reflected.[2] At the same time, a relatively equal amount of energy from the Earth is reradiated back into space. In this activity, the temperature of the air at the Earth's surface is measured. Temperature is the degree of hotness or coldness of matter.

Controlling variables
Meteorologists place their thermometers in a Stevenson Screen, a specially designed white box ventilated on all four sides for air flow. A double roof with air space between the two layers insulates the thermometer from the sun's direct rays. The box is mounted 1.5 meters above a grassy surface, facing north.

To replicate the conditions used by professionals (without the use of the Stevenson Screen), the thermometer should be shaded and situated about 1.5 meters above an open, grassy area. In the absence of grass, choose a level surface typical of the surroundings. Avoid pavement or concrete.

Celsius versus Fahrenheit

The use of the Celsius scale is preferred and encouraged as the one used by the scientific community and most of the world. For comparisons in the *Extension*, use the scale in which temperatures are presently reported (Fahrenheit in the United States). Students should not convert from one scale to the other; all data should be taken directly from measurement readings. The relative values of each scale should be learned through experience.

Official Temperature Reports

Each of the following sources provides regular updates of the official temperatures. **The Weather Channel®** generally gives current local data about every one to eight minutes.

National Weather Service (NWS) reports on **NOAA** (National Oceanic and Atmospheric Administration) **Weather Radio** are broadcast on the weather band (frequencies range from 162.4 to 162.55MHz). These localized reports are updated every one to three hours and repeated every four to six minutes.

Several *Weather Websites* offering current weather data are listed at the back of this book. Some National Weather Service sites have METAR readings, a summary of hourly data for the previous 24 hours or so.

Patterns

Temperature patterns are visually discernable when accumulated data are plotted on a graph. One pattern to observe is the change that takes place hourly, during a single day. Another pattern is the daily high temperature (or the daily temperature at a certain time, say 2:00) over a week. Since line graphs are normally used to show change over time, students transition from the familiar bar graph to the line graph in this activity.

1. Ramsey, Dan. *Weather Forecasting, A Young Meteorologist's Guide.* Tab Books. Blue Ridge Summit, PA. 1990.
2. Williams, Jack. *The Weather Book (USA Today®).* Random House, Inc. New York. 1992.

Management

1. To make valid comparisons, thermometers should either have matching readings or be made equivalent by computation.
2. Students should know how to read a thermometer (*A Matter of Degrees*) and understand variables which need to be controlled (*On Location*). The *Graphing Thermometer* may be used to construct a large class bar graph.
3. Members in groups of two or three can take turns holding the stick, reading the thermometer, and recording the temperature.
4. Make a transparency of the graph to help guide the transition from bar graph to line graph.
5. There are several options for taking temperature readings:

a. Take hourly readings one or more days, using a new page each day.
b. Take temperatures twice each day, morning and afternoon, for a week. Plot the two daily temperatures on the same bar. Then make a line graph using one color for morning and another for afternoon.
c. Take temperatures at solar noon (or a specified afternoon time) each day throughout the year. Make seasonal comparisons.

Rather than giving students the recording page, groups ready for more independent work might:

Open-ended: Plan their own investigation to track temperature patterns during the day or week. How variables are controlled will determine whether the results are meaningful.

Guided planning: Plan their own investigation, with the aid of the following questions:
How will variables be controlled when placing the thermometer?
What temperature scale will be used?
How often will data be collected?
How will the results be recorded?
How will the data be shown? If using a graph, what kind?
How will the data be shared with others?

Procedure

1. Ask the *Key Question*, "How does the temperature change over time?" Record responses on chart paper.
2. Distribute the activity page. Discuss the scale to be used, how often the readings should be done, and variables to be controlled, drawing on students' previous investigations. Have students organize their recording space. A date/time/temperature table is one choice.
3. Instruct each group to attach a thermometer to one end of a stick with tape. This provides a built-in height measure and makes it easier to keep hands away from the thermometer.

4. Outside in the shade, spread the groups apart as much as possible. Direct students to place their sticks upright on the grass with the thermometer at the top. After the thermometer liquid stabilizes, have each group read and record the temperature.
5. Return to the room and assign two groups (for accuracy) to take readings for each interval.
6. After all data are collected, have the groups report their temperature readings for the class to record. Resolve any discrepancies.

7. Use the graph transparency to help students complete the bar graph. Ask questions such as: "How should we label each side of the graph? What were the lowest and highest temperatures? By what should we count so that these numbers fit on the graph? What title should we give the graph?"
8. Instruct students to make a dot in the middle, at the top of each colored bar, and connect the dots with straight lines. Students can now see change over time and how a line and bar graph are related. Have students write their observations of the data.
9. Continue daily temperature readings, at least once a day, as part of an on-going weather station. Add the temperature to your *Station Model.*

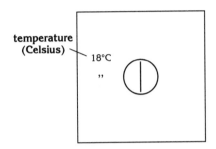

Discussion
1. What variables were controlled when we took temperatures? Why is it important to control them?
2. How would you describe the temperature pattern for today? ...for this week? What kinds of patterns do you notice?
3. When did the temperature change more rapidly? ...more slowly?
4. When were temperatures the warmest? ...the coolest? Why do you think so? Are these the warmest and coolest temperatures for the day? (Encourage students to find out the high and low temperatures for that day and compare to their data, which are limited by being taken only during school hours.)

5. What is the temperature range for ___ (name a day)? [Find the difference between the highest and lowest readings.]
6. How did this week's temperatures affect you?
7. What new question(s) do you have as a result of doing this activity?

 Journal prompt: Based on our data, what temperatures would you predict for tomorrow? How should you dress? Justify your answer.

Extensions
1. After data have accumulated, compare one season with another.
2. Ask the question, "How do our temperature readings compare with official readings for our area? Prepare the second activity page by reproducing a small local map, perhaps from the telephone directory, that includes the nearest reported city and your location. Glue it in the box and make copies of the page.

   Become familiar with the source to be used for official temperatures. Have students take temperature readings every hour—and at the *same* time as official readings. Analyze the data together.

Time	School Temp.	Official Temp.	Difference

Home Link
Keep the data intervals going at home by letting volunteers monitor radio, television, or Internet reports in the evening and morning. Add this data to that taken at school to find when temperatures change most rapidly or most slowly during a 24-hour period.

Connections
The sun heats the land, the water, and the air on and near the Earth. The temperature of the air is what is reported by meteorologists. As students take the air temperature, they are applying previously-gained knowledge about reading thermometers and controlling location variables. Attention has turned to temperature patterns over the course of a day and a week, using a line graph. Continuing these observations over a long period of time will be invaluable for discovering the seasonal cycle of weather changes and eventually connecting these changes to astronomy—the rotation and revolution of the Earth in relation to the sun.

Now let's turn our attention to a location concept with both local and global connotations. Looking at Earth's surface from a distance, two kinds of matter dominate—solid land and liquid water. How these two substances receive and radiate heat, which has major implications for the Earth's weather, is investigated in *Tub Temps.*

Temperature Tally

How does the temperature change over time?

Record the temperatures below.

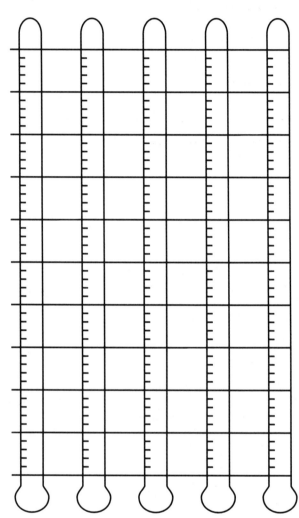

What does the graph tell you?

Temperature Tally

How do our temperature readings compare with official readings for our area?

Map

- On the map, circle the nearest reported city. Mark your location with a box.

- What is the distance between your location and the nearest reported city?

Record your temperature readings and those reported by

_____

source

How do your results compare? If there are differences, what do you think might cause them?

Topics
Heating and cooling of soil versus water
Properties of matter

Key Question
How do the temperatures of soil and water compare over time?

Focus
Students will compare the rate with which soil and water gain and lose heat energy.

Guiding Documents
Project 2061 Benchmarks
- *The sun warms the land, air, and water.*
- *Some materials conduct heat much better than others. Poor conductors can reduce heat loss.*
- *Things change in steady, repetitive, or irregular ways—or sometimes in more than one way at the same time. Often the best way to tell which kinds of change are happening is to make a table or graph of measurements.*

NRC Standards
- *Objects have many observable properties, including size, weight, shape, color, temperature, and the ability to react with other substances. Those properties can be measured using tools, such as rulers, balances, and thermometers.*
- *Earth materials are solid rocks and soil, water, and the gases of the atmosphere. The varied materials have different physical and chemical properties, which make them useful in different ways, for example, as building materials, as sources of fuel, or for growing the plants we use as food. Earth materials provide many of the resources that humans use.*

NCTM Standards 2000*
- *Identify and describe situations with constant or varying rates of change and compare them*
- *Select and apply appropriate standard units and tools to measure length, area, volume, weight, time, temperature, and the size of angles*
- *Represent data using tables and graphs such as line plots, bar graphs, and line graphs*

Math
Measurement
  time
  temperature
Whole number operations
Graphing
  line

Science
Physical science
  properties of matter
  heat energy
Earth science
  meteorology

Integrated Processes
Observing
Predicting
Collecting and recording data
Comparing and contrasting
Controlling variables
Interpreting data
Relating

Materials
2 light-colored buckets or tubs
3 thermometers
Stick, 1-1.5 meters long
Soil
Tool to scoop soil
Water
Crayons or colored pencils

For an optional approach using groups, see materials suggested in *Management 7*.

Background Information
Soil absorbs heat energy faster than water, but also releases it more quickly. Water warms and cools very slowly. A look at the properties of soil and water helps provide the explanation of why this happens.

1) Soil is opaque; water is transparent. The sun's rays pass through transparent materials more readily than opaque materials, distributing the heat energy to greater depths. Since sunlight can't pass through the rough, dark surface of soil, the heat energy is absorbed only at the surface. Have you ever dug into the sand on a hot beach and felt how cool it is underneath?

2) Water, because it is a liquid, moves easily. The water molecules help transport heat to different areas and depths (convection). Soil, a solid, is more stationary and the heat remains at the surface. The heat energy absorbed in land is transferred by contact (conduction).

3) Water has a greater capacity for heat. It takes more heat to raise the temperature of water than it takes to raise the temperature of the same amount of soil. Water is slow to take in heat but then equally stingy about releasing it. Water temperatures vary less over time than soil temperatures.

The different rates with which land and water absorb heat energy affect our weather. The Earth's land masses (soil) and oceans (water) release varying amounts of heat energy into the air above them. This creates air masses with different temperatures. Coastline cities which receive breezes off the ocean will likely have moderate temperatures because water gains and loses heat slowly. Inland cities will generally have greater temperature extremes because the soil will heat quickly during the day and cool rapidly as the sun goes down.

The purposes of this activity are to sharpen students' observation skills as they look at the properties of soil and water, to practice controlling variables as they measure time and temperatures, to produce a line graph which shows change over time, and to interpret the data they have collected. The results of this experience should be related to geography and weather when students are ready to make these connections.

Management
1. Plan to do this activity during a warm time of the year—late spring, summer, or early fall.
2. At least one hour before doing the activity, prepare the containers by filling one about two-thirds full of water and another about two-thirds full of soil. To achieve equal starting temperatures, add hot or cold water until the water temperature matches that of the soil.
3. Find three thermometers with matching readings. To measure air temperature, tape one thermometer to the top of the 1 to 1.5 meter stick. Air temperature should be taken in the shade over a grassy surface at a height of about 1.5 meters.
4. To avoid having the thermometers register the sun's radiation during the sun readings, put them in the tubs just long enough to stabilize, temporarily shade them with pieces of paper, and measure. Then remove the thermometers.
5. Take an equal number of readings in the sun and the shade, not counting starting temperature. Plan for at least a two-hour block of time during the heat of the day.

	Time	Soil Temp. (°__)	Water Temp. (°__)
Start	12:30		
Sun	12:45		
	1:00		
	1:15		
	1:30		
Shade	1:45		
	2:00		
	2:15		
	2:30		

6. Always read thermometers at eye level, without removing the bulb from the soil or water.
7. To do this activity in small groups, transparent containers with a wide opening such as liter boxes or pint jars can be substituted for the buckets or tubs. Each group will need a set of the remaining materials listed.

Procedure
1. Put the two buckets, one with water and one with soil, in a place where students can gather and observe. Have them use their senses, particularly sight and touch, to describe each kind of matter.
2. Distribute the first activity page and have them record their descriptions.
3. Ask students to predict which will warm up faster, soil or water, or if they will warm up at the same speed. They should also comment on which material will cool down faster. Ask for reasons on which the students base their predictions, then have them write the predictions.
4. Discuss how often to take the temperatures (every 10, 15, 20, 25, or 30 minutes) and have students record the time interval.
5. Since temperature varies at different depths, instruct students to place the thermometer bulb at the same depth each time, about 3 or 4 cm.
6. Take the class outside to a grassy spot with both sun and shade. Measure the air, soil, and water temperatures in the shade. Have students describe and record the weather—wind, clouds, and air temperature. Direct them to also record the time, starting soil and water temperatures, and the temperature scale (°C or °F).
7. Remove the thermometers from the containers and place the soil and water in a grassy, sunny spot. Go indoors.
8. Return outside a few minutes before the next reading. Have students put one thermometer in each container so that the thermometer faces away from the sun. After a few minutes, when the thermometers have stabilized, direct students to record the soil and water temperatures.

9. Remove the two thermometers and repeat the temperature readings at regular intervals throughout the afternoon. After taking several sun readings, move the containers into the shade and continue readings at the same time intervals. For shade readings, the thermometers may be left in the containers.

10. Ask students how to find the temperature range of soil. [Subtract the lowest from the highest soil temperatures.] Repeat for water and record on the activity page.

11. Distribute the line graph. Have students label the vertical axis (°__), the horizontal axis (time), and give the graph a title. Discuss how to determine the temperature range and increments to be used.

12. Instruct students to complete the key and plot the data using two colors, one for soil and another for water.

13. Discuss the results and have students write what they have discovered.

Discussion

1. How would you describe the soil? [rough, dark, dull, solid, opaque, etc.] How would you describe the water? [smooth, shiny, transparent, liquid, etc.]

2. What variables did we control? [time intervals and depth the thermometer was placed]

3. How much did the soil's temperature change? (Find the temperature range: highest minus lowest temperature) How much did the water's temperature change?

4. Look at your graph. What patterns do you notice? [Examples: The temperature climbs sharply at first and then slows. It also drops sharply when first put into the shade. The soil temperature got warmer than the water temperature. *The Big Idea*: Water heats and cools more slowly than soil.]

5. What do you think might happen to the temperature of the air right above the soil? [Heat energy released from the soil would make air temperatures heat up quickly in the sun and cool down quickly in the shade.] What do you think might happen to the temperature of the air right above the water? [The air temperature wouldn't change as much as it did above the soil.] See *Extension 3*.

6. Why don't you go swimming the first warm day of spring? [You will want to wait several days or weeks since it takes time for the water to absorb enough heat to make swimming a comfortable experience.]

7. Is your location surrounded by land or is there a large body of water nearby? Would you expect greater or smaller differences between the high and low temperatures of the day? [for land, greater differences; for water, smaller differences] Why? [because land gains and loses heat energy more rapidly than water]

Extensions

1. Measure and graph air temperatures along with soil and water temperatures at each time interval.

2. Design an investigation to compare the temperatures of soil and water at different depths.

3. Compare air temperatures 1 or 2 cm above soil and water over time.

* Reprinted with permission from *Principles and Standards for School Mathematics,* 2000 by the National Council of Teachers of Mathematics. All rights reserved.

Connections

The differences in heat gain and loss in these small samples of soil and water inform you about the weather and climate at your location. Time is introduced as another variable affecting temperature. Inland areas usually have greater temperature extremes from day to night and from season to season because land absorbs and loses heat energy quickly. Locations along an ocean usually have more moderate daily and seasonal temperatures.

Later, when students are developmentally ready, this activity forms the basis for generalizing temperature differences in soil and water to the large masses of land and oceans on the Earth. Together with global wind patterns, this will help give them the bigger picture of weather. Middle school standards from both NRC and Project 2061 speak to the major influence of the heat energy held in the oceans on climate.

Let's build on the foundational discoveries about land and water by looking at broader temperature patterns in *Nationwide Highs*. How does location on a larger scale affect temperature?

Tub Temps

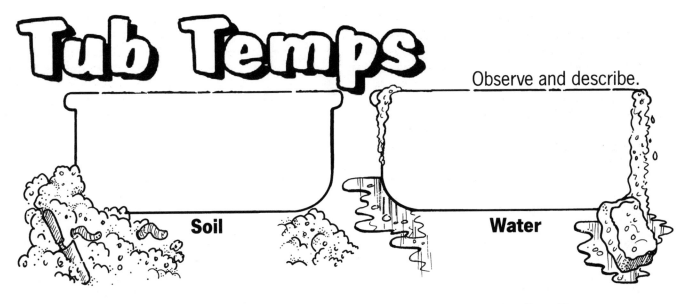

Observe and describe.

Soil　　　　**Water**

How do the temperatures of soil and water compare over time?

Prediction:

Weather:

Time interval:
Thermometer depth:

	Time	Soil Temp. (°__)	Water Temp. (°__)
Start			
Sun			
Shade			

Soil Temperature Range　　　Water Temperature Range

Tub Temps

Line Graph

Key

What did you discover?

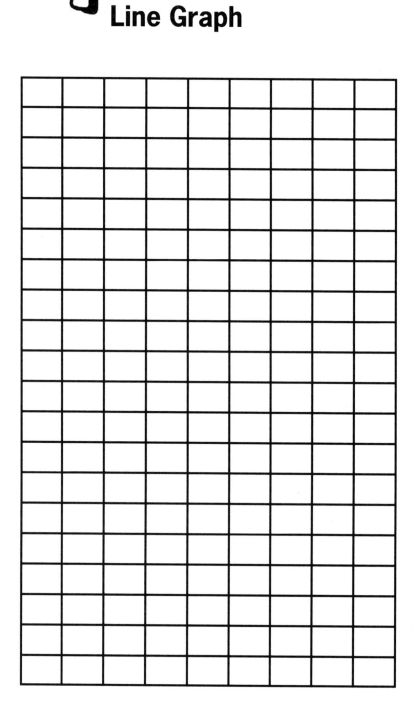

NATIONWIDE HIGHS

Topic
United States temperature patterns

Key Questions
1. How will my chosen city's temperature change during the week?
2. How do temperatures around the United States compare?

Focus
Each student will track the high temperature of a city for a week, post the daily information on a large United States map using a color-coded key, and observe the temperature patterns of their city as well as of the country.

Guiding Documents
Project 2061 Benchmarks
- *Geometric figures, number sequences, graphs, diagrams, sketches, number lines, maps, and stories can be used to represent objects, events, and processes in the real world, although such representations can never be exact in every detail.*
- *Add, subtract, multiply, and divide whole numbers mentally, on paper, and with a calculator.*

NRC Standard
- *Weather changes from day to day and over the seasons. Weather can be described by measurable quantities, such as temperature, wind direction and speed, and precipitation.*

NCTM Standards 2000*
- *Develop fluency in adding, subtracting, multiplying, and dividing whole numbers*
- *Represent data using tables and graphs such as line plots, bar graphs, and line graphs*
- *Use representations to model and interpret physical, social, and mathematical phenomena*

Math
Statistics
Mental computation
Graphing
   broken-line and bar

Science
Earth science
   meteorology

Social Science
Geography
   United States

Integrated Processes
Observing
Predicting
Collecting and recording data
Comparing and contrasting
Inferring
Relating

Materials
Large United States map on bulletin board
Pushpins or straight pins
2" white paper squares, 1 per student
10 colors of paper, 1½" x 2" (see *Management 2*)
10 small envelopes (see *Management 2*)
Black crayon or felt-tip pen
Newspaper weather section

Background Information
Many factors affect the temperatures of cities. One is latitude. During the winter, United States cities in the higher latitudes tend to be cooler than cities in latitudes closer to the Equator. But latitude alone does not determine temperature. Higher elevations tend to be cooler than lower elevations. The prevailing direction of winds also affects temperature. Are the winds coming from the ocean or blowing over land? The prevailing wind pattern in the United States is from west to east. Because water absorbs and releases heat energy more slowly than land, a West Coast city which receives breezes off the ocean generally has more moderate temperatures than the extremes experienced in the Great Plains.

At this stage, students do not necessarily need to be exposed to and understand all of these factors. It is enough that they see general temperature patterns and start to ask questions about why there are differences. This activity is a means to stimulate their curiosity.

Through the study of temperature patterns in cities around the United States, students can gain a feel for geographical locations, a broader picture of the seasons, and a sense of change over time along with some practice in mental computation. There is a natural integration of geography, science, and mathematics as well as an opportunity to sharpen thinking skills.

Management

1. Mount the United States map—or country or state of your choice—on a large bulletin board.

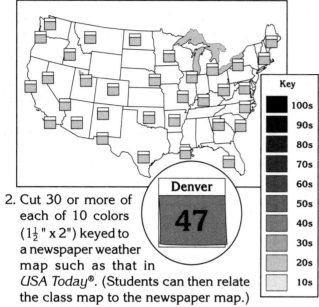

2. Cut 30 or more of each of 10 colors ($1\frac{1}{2}$" x 2") keyed to a newspaper weather map such as that in *USA Today*®. (Students can then relate the class map to the newspaper map.) Alternatively, ten colors of small sticky notes may be used. Deposit each color in a separate envelope. Make a key with each color representing a 10-degree range.

3. Cut the 2" white paper squares. The city name will be written at the top and the appropriate color with temperature will be attached over the remaining part.

4. As temperatures are removed from the map, have students put them in the appropriate envelope. On succeeding days, students can search among the "recycled" temperatures first before writing new ones.

5. Newspapers report national and state temperature highs for the previous day. Use the scale in which they are reported, presently Fahrenheit. Options for data collection include bringing in multiple copies of the newspaper weather section each day, posting one newspaper for students to consult, making multiple copies of the data, or making a transparency. If you wish, data can be gathered ahead of time by saving newspapers from the previous week.

6. To ensure a geographically representative sample and that newspaper data are available, pre-select the cities that will be graphed. Choose cities from different latitudes and with varying environments (proximity to the ocean, mountainous, desert, etc.) Write the city names on paper scraps, one per student, for a drawing.

7. Pick a current weather-related story from the newspaper to introduce the activity.

8. Most cities will have high temperatures above zero, but an occasional dip below zero is a good computational challenge as students determine the amount of change.

9. Plan to do this activity during two or more different seasons, with winter being one. To extend the investigation, use the second activity page for recording and comparing seasonal temperatures.

Procedure

1. Read a weather-related story that is currently in the news. Ask, "Where do you think this place is? Do you think other places close to this city have the same temperature? How about cities around the country?"

2. Encourage students to make some predictions. Ask, "Where do you think it will be warm? Where do you think it will be cool?"

3. Have each student draw a city name you have pre-selected and record it on the activity page you distribute as well as the top of a 2" white square.

4. Direct students to find their city's high temperature for the *previous* day, record it on the page and on the appropriate color of paper, and pin the city name with its temperature on the United States map.

5. Guide a time of observation and discussion.

6. Have students update their city information each day by posting the new high temperature from the previous day and saying to the class, "My city went up (or down) ___ degrees."

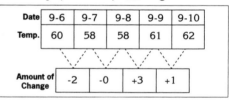

Date	9-6	9-7	9-8	9-9	9-10
Temp.	60	58	58	61	62
Amount of Change		-2	-0	+3	+1

7. Hold a short discussion each day about the changes and new observations.

8. Instruct students to complete the broken-line graph by writing the degree increments and dates, marking and connecting the temperatures of their city, and giving the graph a title.

9. Have students take turns playing "What city am I?" at the end of the week. Since students will likely know who had what city, collect the activity pages and redistribute them randomly. A student might say, "This city started the week at 60°. The pattern it followed was -2, -0, +3, +1. What city am I?"

As each change in temperature is announced, have the other students compute the change mentally and, at the same time, demonstrate the pattern by moving their hands higher or lower. Then they should look at the large map to find a city with the ending temperature which, in the example, would be 62°. If more than one city qualifies, all the possibilities should be mentioned.

60°   -2   -0   +3   +1
Hand Motions

Discussion

1. How did your city's temperature change from yesterday? (+ or - how many degrees)
2. What is the most common temperature band (color) today?
3. What is the difference between the highest and lowest reported temperatures? Do you think there were any other cities higher than the highest temperature on our map? [Yes.] Why? [Because the newspaper reports only some of the cities in the U.S.]
4. For what place do you wish there were a temperature reading? (Use the Internet to find that information.)
5. Which cities are temperature twins? What, if anything, do they have in common?
6. What pairs of cities close to each other have the greatest difference in temperature? How might their difference be explained? What would you want to know to help you explain the difference? [the cities' elevations, direction of the prevailing winds, distance between the two cities, etc.]
7. How would you describe the location of the coldest cities? [northern, southern, eastern, or western part of the country; high elevation or low elevation (if known); close to ocean or inland; etc.] How about the location of the warmest cities?
8. What changes do you notice between yesterday's and today's temperature map? (Example: A new color was added today because one city's temperature dropped to a lower level than any city yesterday.)
9. What does the broken-line graph tell about your city?
10. How is our class map like the newspaper temperature map? (If the same color key is used, the 10-degree colored temperature bands should be in the same general locations.)

Extensions

1. Have students use the second activity page to track and compare high temperatures for their chosen city during two or more seasons. Instruct them to determine the five-day averages—mean or median—and illustrate the averages with a bar graph. Compare to other cities.
   Questions:
   • What did you notice about the temperatures of your city during different seasons? (Examples: My city had similar temperatures in fall and spring. The temperatures did not change much all year in my city.)
   • Which cities had the greatest differences in high temperatures? Where are they located?
   • Which cities had the least differences in high temperatures? Where are they located? [probably in Hawaii or along the West Coast, places moderated by the ocean and wind direction]
2. Encourage each student to research his or her city and construct a travel or informational brochure about it.
3. Have students determine the latitude and longitude of their cities.

Curriculum Correlation
Literature

The following books from the *Imagine Living Here* series by Vicki Cobb (Walker and Company, New York) give a feel for two kinds of environments in the United States—the weather, the daily and seasonal lives of people, plants, animals, etc. Suitable for the intermediate grades.
   This Place is Cold. (Alaska) 1989.
   This Place is Dry. (Arizona's Sonoran Desert) 1989.

Home Link

Students with relatives or pen pals in other cities may want to track those cities' temperatures on their own.

* Reprinted with permission from *Principles and Standards for School Mathematics*, 2000 by the National Council of Teachers of Mathematics. All rights reserved.

Connections

As we move from a local to a national picture of temperature, further evidence of the unequal heating of the Earth is amassing. Latitude has now been observed as another factor in temperature differences. Later, when students are better able to truly comprehend the rotation and revolution of the Earth in relation to the sun, the understanding of why this is so will become clearer.

The use of the United States map has already caused students to observe temperature patterns related to location. This naturally progresses to a study of isotherms in the next activity, *Heat Bands.*

NATIONWIDE HIGHS

Welcome to . . .

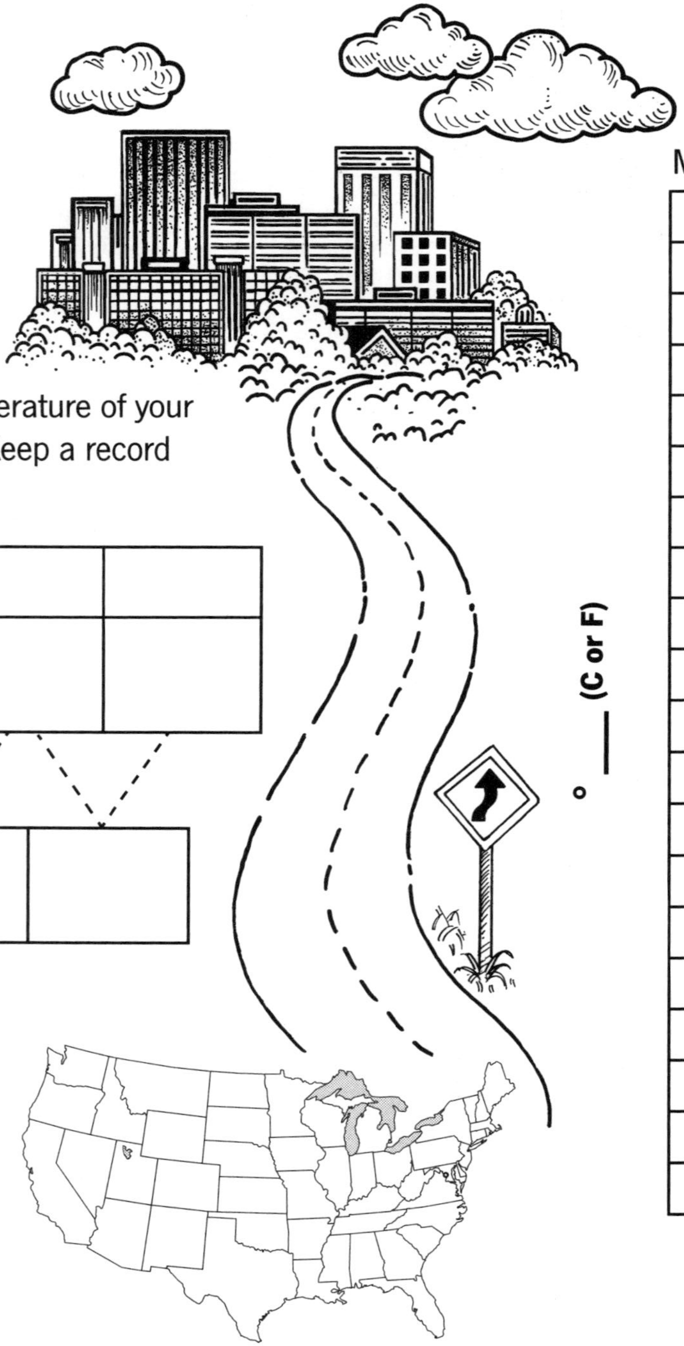

On a large U.S. map, display the high temperature of your chosen city. Tell how it changes each day. Keep a record below, then make a broken-line graph.

Date					
Temp. ° __(C or F)__					

Amount of Change

What city am I?

Read the temperature pattern for the week and have others guess the city.

Make a line graph of the temperatures.

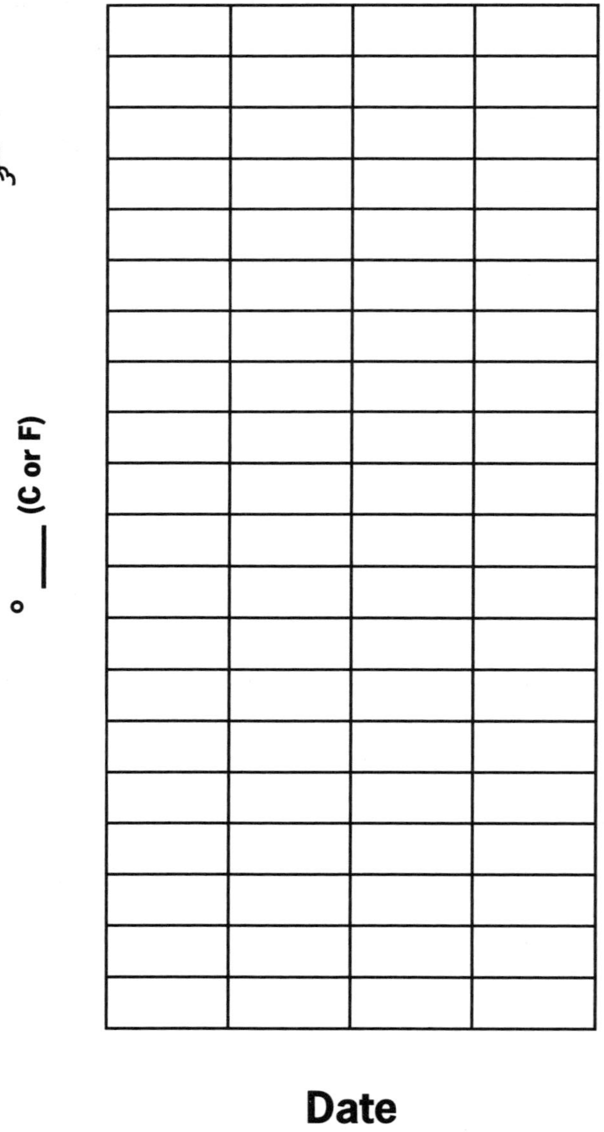

° _____ (C or F)

Date

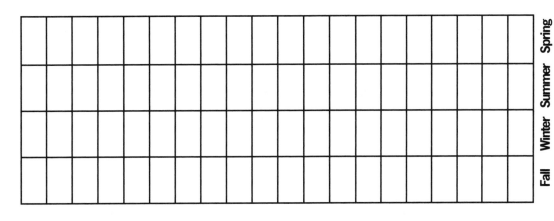

NATIONWIDE HIGHS

Comparing Seasons

Welcome to . . .

Record your chosen city's high temperature for five days each season.

Illustrate the average temperatures with a bar graph.

Fall		Winter		Summer		Spring	
Date	Temp.	Date	Temp.	Date	Temp.	Date	Temp.
Average Temp.							

_____ °

How do the seasonal temperatures compare?

Season: Fall   Winter   Summer   Spring

Season

Heat Bands

Topic
Temperature patterns: isotherms

Key Questions
How can a map be turned into a temperature graph?
How does geographical location affect temperature?

Focus
Students will interpret an isotherm map based on increments of ten, noticing temperature patterns related to latitude. For those who are ready, opportunity is given to learn how to draw isotherms using data they gather.

Guiding Documents
Project 2061 Benchmarks
- *Graphical display of numbers may make it possible to spot patterns that are not otherwise obvious, such as comparative size and trends.*
- *Geometric figures, number sequences, graphs, diagrams, sketches, number lines, maps, and stories can be used to represent objects, events, and processes in the real world, although such representations can never be exact in every detail.*

NRC Standard
- *Weather changes from day to day and over the seasons. Weather can be described by measurable quantities, such as temperature, wind direction and speed, and precipitation.*

NCTM Standards 2000*
- *Represent data using tables and graphs such as line plots, bar graphs, and line graphs*
- *Describe the shape and important features of a set of data and compare related data sets, with an emphasis on how the data are distributed*

National Geography Standards
- *Show spatial information on geographic representations*
- *Obtain information on the characteristics of places (e.g., climate, elevation, and population density) by interpreting maps*

Math
Number sense
    ranges
Spatial sense
Graphing

Science
Earth science
    meteorology

Social Science
Geography
    United States (adaptable to other countries)

Integrated Processes
Observing
Collecting and recording data
Comparing and contrasting
Interpreting data
Relating

Materials
Crayons or colored pencils (see *Management 1*)
Temperature data from newspaper
Globe

Background Information
On television weather reports, in the newspaper, and online, students have seen weather maps banded by isotherms, lines of equal temperature. This activity focuses first on interpreting an isotherm map, then on the more challenging skill of gathering data and drawing isotherms.

Isolines is the general name for lines of equal value. Specific names are given for specialized data: isotherms (temperature), isobars (barometric pressure), isohumes (humidity), and so on.

An isotherm map is actually a specialized kind of graph, a graph being "a pictorial device used to display numerical relationships." Microclimates, such as the classroom, can be mapped with 1-degree isotherms. More commonly, isotherm maps with 10-degree increments represent the temperatures of large land masses, whether whole continents such as Europe, Africa, and South America or large countries such as Canada, Australia, and the United States.

Isotherm maps show the relationship of geographical locations—latitude, proximity to large bodies of water or land—with temperature. With further research, location factors such as elevation, mountains, and other physical features can deepen the connections.

Management

1. Choose a color scheme for the key. Consider coordinating it to your local paper or the *USA Today*® isotherm key. Find an assortment of crayons or colored pencils that matches the key. Several shades of blues, greens, and oranges are often necessary.

below zero	0s	10s	20s	30s	40s	50s	60s	70s	80s	90s	100s

2. Because U.S. temperatures are presently reported in Fahrenheit, use that scale.
3. Since interpreting and drawing isotherms are likely a new experience, working with a partner may help students gain confidence. The whole class will be involved in gathering and sharing data with each other in *Part Two*.
4. Collect several copies of the weather section of the local newspaper or *USA Today*® for two consecutive days. They do not have to be the current issues but should be recent ones.
5. Emphasis is on drawing an isotherm *between* two temperatures rather than being concerned that it should be closer to one than the other. If, for example, there are temperatures of 58 and 65, the 60s isotherm need not be drawn closer to 58 than to 65. In fact, more data would be needed to fine-tune the line positions. The focus is instead on the general picture. Drawings will vary somewhat from person to person.
6. Be aware of several guidelines when drawing isotherms:
   a. Isotherms should be drawn in relation to city points, not to the position of the city name or the temperature number.
   b. The lines should be drawn *through* any city point with a "tens" temperature such as 40 or 50.
   c. Isotherms must be consecutive, either up or down one from its neighbor. If one city is in the 50s and a neighboring city is in the 70s, a 60s isotherm must be inserted between them.
   d. Isotherms should begin and end at the map's boundary lines.
   e. There can be more than one of the same isotherm on a given map.
7. This activity can easily be adapted to other countries by substituting a map of the continent or country (if it has at least three temperature bands) for the final page in *Part Two*.

Procedure

Part One: Interpreting isotherms

1. Hold up a newspaper with an isotherm map. Ask, "Does anyone recognize this map? What does it show? Where else have you seen one?" [television weather report, weather website, etc.] Explain that the colored bands represent a 10-degree temperature range. Point to one of the bands, as an example, and tell the class all the cities in this band had temperatures in the ____ (50s or whatever is appropriate). The lines separating the bands are lines of equal temperature called isotherms. (Point to one line.) Along this line, the temperatures are 50 degrees. (Point to another line.) This is the 60-degree isotherm. So temperatures between 50 and 60 are in this band.

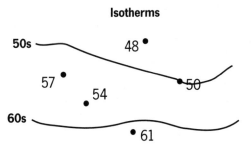

Isotherms

2. Give students the first map, with the isotherms drawn. Guide the coloring of the isotherm key according to the color scheme you have chosen (see *Management 1*).
3. Model how to color each city point, using the isotherm key as a guide. This procedure helps students better see how the bands were constructed and prepares them for drawing their own maps. Then have them fill in the bands completely with color.
4. Study the map together. Use the discussion questions to guide interpretation.
5. Follow up by having student groups examine two consecutive newspaper temperature maps, noticing repeated patterns and changes. The same discussion questions can be used.

Part Two: Drawing isotherms (for those students who are ready)

1. Distribute the page with two practice maps and instruct students to color the key and city points of the upper map as they did in *Part One*.
2. Encourage students to look at places where the city colors change and draw a line between those areas, from map boundary to map boundary, until all the temperature areas have been defined. Circulate to provide assistance as needed.
3. Have students color the city points on the lower map, an island. Newburg (74) and Greenfield (92) have no 80s temperature between them so guide students through the drawing of both an 80s and a 90s isotherm. They should notice there are two

80s isotherms or, in another way of looking at it, two bands of 70s.

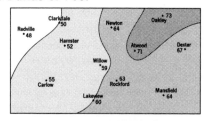

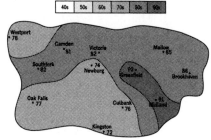

4. Bring in newspaper temperature data, which will be the previous day's highs, and instruct students to write the temperatures by each city on the United States map provided or a continent or country map of your choice.
5. Have students color-code the city points, draw the isotherms, and color the temperature bands.
6. Discuss the patterns.

Discussion
Part One
1. What is the range of temperatures on this map? [40s to 90s]
2. Trace (or point to) the 60s isotherm with your finger. [second isotherm from the top]
3. Name some other cities in the same temperature band as ours. What do the locations of these cities have in common? [roughly similar latitudes]
4. Which temperature band covers the most area? ...the least area?
5. Which part of the country is warmest? ...coolest? [Warmer locations—the lower latitudes—are generally closer to the Equator which receives the sun's most direct rays. The higher latitudes, further from the Equator, tend to be cooler; the sun's rays are more indirect. (Use a globe to help students see the relationship.)]

6. What other temperature patterns do you notice? [There is a hot spot in southern Arizona and California. There is a north-south band of cooler temperatures along the West Coast, but it is warmer inland in California. The East Coast does not have a similar north-south cool temperature band. (Recognition of patterns is sufficient. The "why" requires more advanced knowledge of global wind patterns and the physical geography of the West and East Coasts. Students would also need to transfer learning from the *Tub Temps* investigation to national geography, a task more developmentally appropriate to the middle-school level.)]

Part Two
1. What was the easiest part about drawing this map? What was the most difficult?
2. What patterns do you notice on this map?
3. How does the map you drew compare to the one in the newspaper? (Students should have a feeling of accomplishment as they recognize similar patterns. Differences will arise because the newspaper is most likely using predicted rather than actual data and because its data are more extensive. To compare like data, yesterday's highs mapped by students would correspond to the newspaper forecast map from the day before yesterday.)

Extension
Save several newspaper temperature maps or student-drawn maps from different seasons. Have students compare the maps from two seasons, noting what has changed (temperature range) and what is similar (latitude patterns).

Curriculum Correlation
Technology
Have students investigate websites for isotherm maps of current weather conditions for their location and elsewhere in the world. See *Weather Websites* at the back of this book for suggestions.

Connections
We have found that, at a particular location such as a school site, temperature varies. Isotherm maps show, on a larger scale, that the Earth heats unequally. Geographical location affects temperature. Latitudes closer to the Equator are warmer because they receive more of the sun's direct rays. This could lead to further study of the relationship between the sun and the Earth over the course of the year, why we have seasons.

In the meantime, it is time to assess what students have learned about the bigger picture of how location influences temperature.

Heat Bands

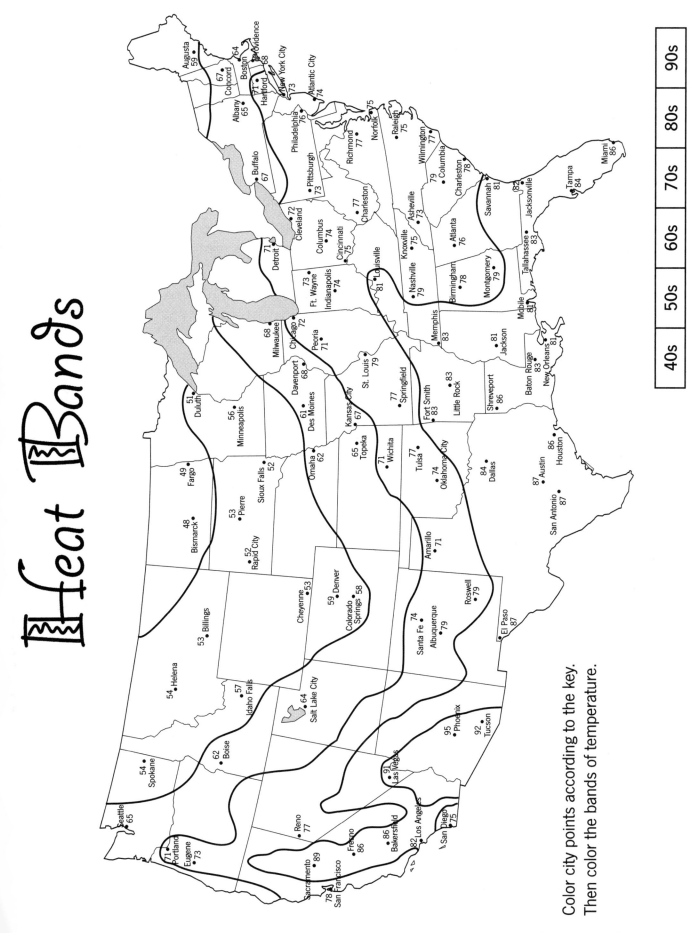

Color city points according to the key.
Then color the bands of temperature.

40s	50s	60s	70s	80s	90s

Augusta 59
Concord 67
Providence
Boston 64
Hartford 71
New York City 68
Atlantic City 74
Albany 65
Philadelphia 76
Pittsburgh 73
Norfolk 75
Raleigh 75
Richmond 77
Wilmington 77
Buffalo 67
Columbia 78
Cleveland 72
Charleston 77
Asheville 73
Charleston 78
Savannah 81
Jacksonville 82
Tampa 84
Miami 86
Columbus 74
Cincinnati 75
Knoxville 75
Atlanta 76
Detroit 71
Louisville 81
Nashville 79
Birmingham 78
Montgomery 79
Tallahassee 83
Ft. Wayne 73
Indianapolis 74
Mobile 81
Milwaukee 68
Chicago 72
Peoria 71
Memphis 83
Jackson 81
Davenport 68
St. Louis 79
Springfield 77
Little Rock 83
Shreveport 86
Baton Rouge 83
New Orleans 81
Duluth 51
Minneapolis 56
Des Moines 61
Kansas City 67
Fort Smith 83
Fargo 49
Sioux Falls 52
Omaha 62
Topeka 65
Wichita 71
Tulsa 77
Oklahoma City 74
Dallas 84
Austin 87
Houston 86
Pierre 53
San Antonio 87
Bismarck 48
Rapid City 52
Amarillo 71
Billings 53
Cheyenne 53
Denver 59
Colorado Springs 58
Roswell 79
El Paso 87
Helena 54
Idaho Falls 57
Salt Lake City 64
Santa Fe 74
Albuquerque 79
Phoenix 95
Tucson 92
Boise 62
Spokane 54
Las Vegas 91
Seattle 65
Reno 77
Fresno 86
Bakersfield 86
Los Angeles 82
San Diego 75
Portland 71
Eugene 73
Sacramento 89
San Francisco 78

Heat Bands

Color the city points using the key. Draw the isotherms. Color the temperature bands.

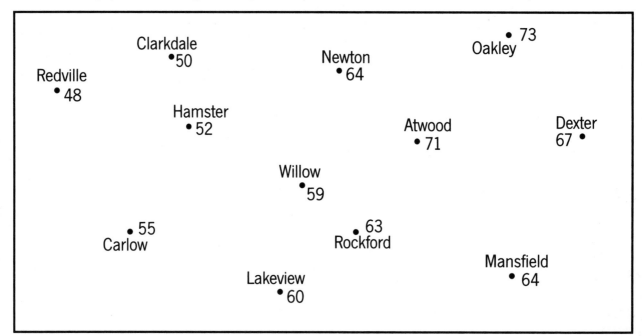

Clarkdale
•50

Newton
•64

Oakley
• 73

Redville
• 48

Hamster
• 52

Atwood
• 71

Dexter
67 •

Willow
•59

• 55
Carlow

• 63
Rockford

Mansfield
• 64

Lakeview
• 60

40s	50s	60s	70s	80s	90s

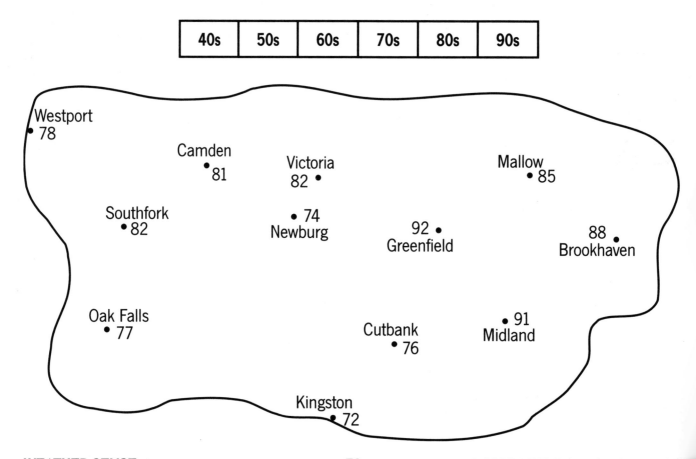

Westport
• 78

Camden
• 81

Victoria
82 •

Mallow
• 85

Southfork
• 82

• 74
Newburg

92 •
Greenfield

88 •
Brookhaven

Oak Falls
• 77

Cutbank
• 76

• 91
Midland

Kingston
• 72

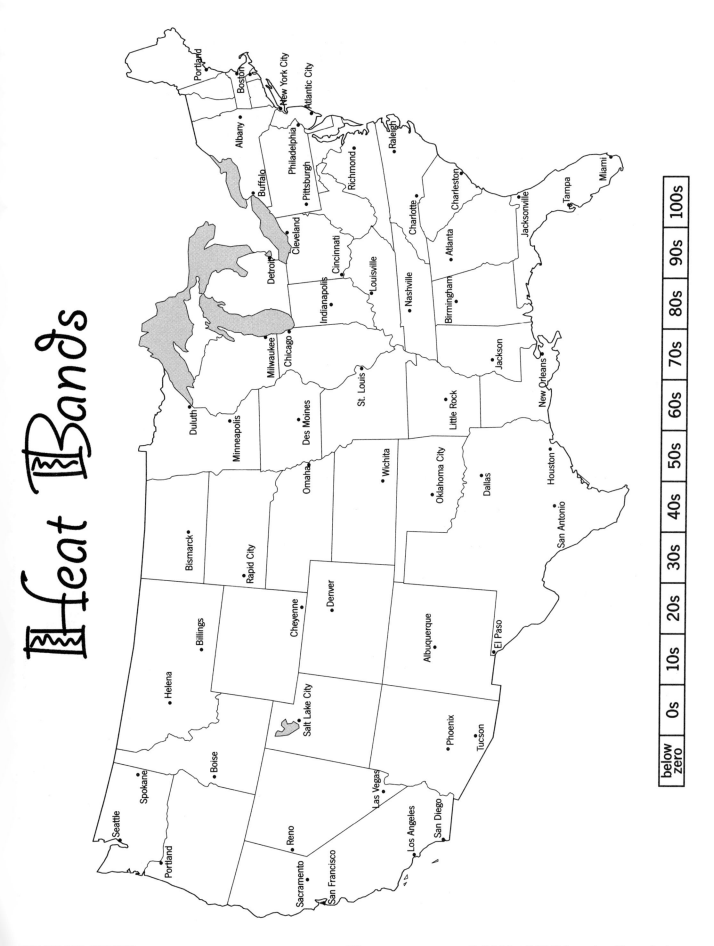

Heat Bands

below zero	0s	10s	20s	30s	40s	50s	60s	70s	80s	90s	100s

Temperature

Essential Question
How does location affect temperature?

Learning Goals
- Observe and gather evidence that temperature varies with location, both locally and globally.

Locally:
- Explore how local variables—sun exposure, surface, distance from, etc.—affect temperature.
- Identify possible school weather station sites where these variables will be controlled.

Globally:
- Investigate differences in the way land and water absorb and emit the sun's heat energy, contributing to unequal heating.
- Gather and plot continental temperature data to discover unequal heating patterns related to latitude.

Global Temperature Assessment

Activity
Give students the travel brochure page. Have them apply learning gained from the temperature activities dealing with latitude by identifying the city that matches each brochure.

Discussion
1. Which city matches each brochure? [left—Bismarck; right—Tucson]
2. What information helped you identify each city? [summer temperatures, location on the map, description of the area, what I know about temperatures at different latitudes, etc.]

Evidence of Learning
Students should use context clues, temperature information, and geographic knowledge to determine that the farm community is in the northern part of the United States. They should reason that the summer temperatures are quite mild compared to those in the second brochure so the city must be in a latitude further from the Equator. Farming and ranching being key industries would eliminate other potential cities such as Salt Lake City and St. Louis, leaving Bismarck as the matching city.

The second brochure shows hot summer temperatures, indicating a location closer to the Equator. The description of the desert environment should narrow the search to the southwest and the city of Tucson.

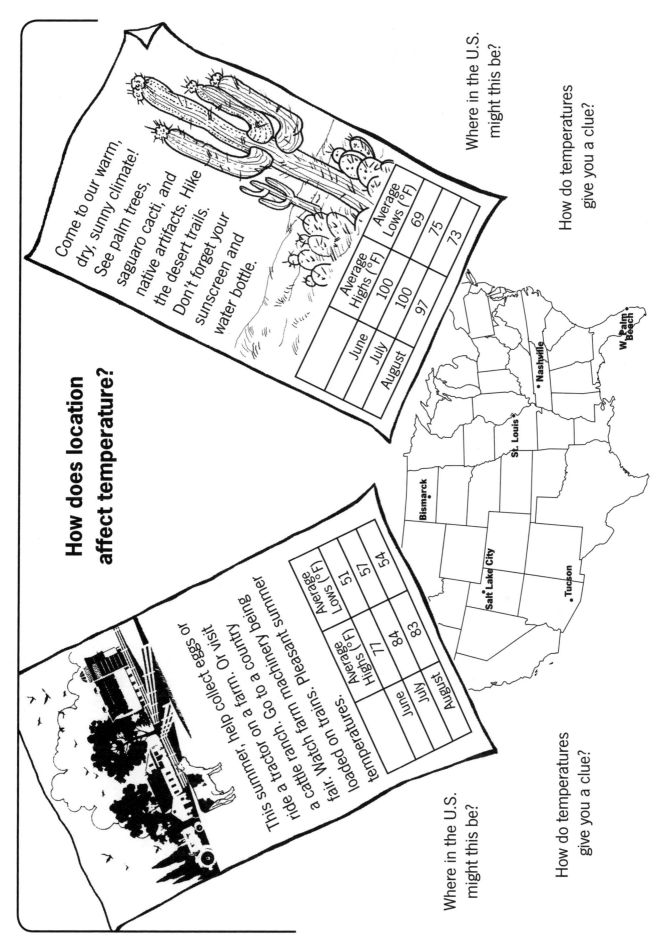

How does location affect temperature?

Come to our warm, dry, sunny climate! See palm trees, saguaro cacti, and native artifacts. Hike the desert trails. Don't forget your sunscreen and water bottle.

	Average Highs (°F)	Average Lows (°F)
June	100	69
July	100	75
August	97	73

This summer, on a farm, ride a tractor, help collect eggs or visit a cattle ranch. Watch farm machinery loaded on trains. Pleasant summer temperatures. Go to a country being a fair.

	Average Highs (°F)	Average Lows (°F)
June	77	51
July	84	57
August	83	54

Where in the U.S. might this be?

How do temperatures give you a clue?

Where in the U.S. might this be?

How do temperatures give you a clue?

Air *and* Air Pressure
Background for the Teacher

The Atmosphere

The Earth is surrounded by the atmosphere, an invisible combination of gases (78% nitrogen, 21% oxygen, and 1% trace gases), held in place by the force of gravity. Scientists have identified layers of atmosphere, partially defined by their temperature patterns. The layer touching the Earth is the *troposphere*. It is about 8 kilometers (5 miles) thick at the Poles and about 19 kilometers (12 miles) thick at the Equator. The world's weather takes place in the troposphere.

Properties of Air

Matter, whether solid, liquid, or gas, has certain identifiable properties. Since air is invisible, we often observe its properties through the effect air has on other matter.

Air takes up space. It fills spaces not filled by other matter. Consider marbles packed in a jar. The space left between marbles, due to their spherical shape, is filled with air. An empty jar isn't really empty; it is filled with air.

Air has weight. Compare the weight of an unfilled basketball and an inflated one. The inflated basketball weighs more than the uninflated one. Air is not very heavy, but it does have weight. One liter of air, at sea level and at a temperature of 20°C, weighs about 1.2 grams.

Although, technically, a balance is used to determine mass, it can be used to show weight comparison qualitatively. In order to determine that air has weight, the air must be compressed into something such as a balloon. Uncompressed air, such as that captured in a plastic bag, cannot be weighed in air because the pressure inside and outside the bag pushes equally; there is no force which causes the balance to move. However, when air is squeezed into a balloon, it has greater pressure than the air surrounding the balloon. If the compressed air is released from one of two balloons balanced on a lever, the air continues to escape until the pressures inside and outside the balloon have reached equilibrium. This causes a change in the position of the balance, showing that air has weight.

Air exerts pressure. Pressure is defined as force per unit area. Air pressure is the weight of air per unit of area. Air must have weight in order to exert pressure. At sea level, air presses with a force of 10 newtons (2.2 pounds) per square centimeter or 14.7 pounds per square inch. At sea level, that force is roughly equivalent to the weight of 10 cars (22,000 pounds) pressing on one square meter! We do not feel the pressure because 1) we live in an ocean of air that is pressing on us equally in all directions and because 2) the tissues, fluids, and air within our bodies are pressing back against the outside air.

Since air pressure is one of the key elements of weather, let's look at it more closely.

Air Pressure

Air Pressure

Air is a gas. In the atmosphere, less dense or thinly spread air exerts lower pressure; more dense or tightly packed air exerts higher pressure. Air with high pressure moves toward air with low pressure in an effort to bring the pressure differences into balance.

Air pressure is an important indicator of weather changes. In a *high-pressure system* in the Northern Hemisphere, a mass of cold air warms and dries as it descends, developing a clockwise-spiraling motion outward toward lower pressure outside the mass. Usually this results in fair weather. The spiraling motion is counterclockwise in the Southern Hemisphere.

High-pressure system

Low-pressure system

In a *low-pressure system,* the surface air flows counterclockwise toward the center where, having no other place to go, it rises. The rising air cools, and with sufficient moisture, forms clouds and possibly precipitation. Low pressure is often indicative of cooler or stormy weather. In the Southern Hemisphere, this motion is clockwise.

Changes in air pressure are measured with a barometer. The mercury barometer, invented by Evangelista Torricelli in 1643, has about a 30-inch glass tube filled with mercury. The mercury rises or falls according to the amount of air pressure. The aneroid barometer—*aneroid* meaning "without liquid"—has a flexible, accordion-like metal in a tightly sealed chamber from which some of the air has been removed. Air pressure causes the metal to contract or expand, moving a pointer along a scale.

In the United States, air pressure is commonly reported in inches, as in inches of mercury. Meteorologists, however, measure air pressure in millibars.

Air pressure patterns are represented on maps with isobars, lines of equal pressure. The closer the isobars, the stronger the winds. The winds might be warm like the Santa Ana winds of Southern California or they may bring cool, stormy weather.

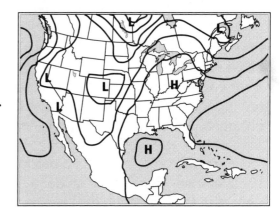

Elevation and Pressure

Air pressure changes with elevation. The higher the elevation, the lesser the weight of the air that is pressing on you. Standard pressure at sea level is 1013 millibars or 29.92 inches. For elevations lower than two or three thousand feet, as a general rule, the air pressure will drop about 1 inch (of mercury) for each 1000-foot rise in altitude or 1 millibar for each 8-meter rise in altitude.

Altitude	Air Pressure
7200 m (38,016 ft)	200 mb (jet stream)
5500 m (18,000 ft)	500 mb
3000 m (9900 ft)	700 mb
1500 m (4950 ft)	850 mb
Sea level	1013 mb

Temperature and Pressure

Air pressure also changes with temperature. The unequal heating of the Earth, due to the Earth's seasonally-changing position in relation to the sun and to the differing heat absorption rates of water and land, causes pressure differences. Where the Earth receives more of the sun's energy, such as at the Equator, the air warms up. This warm, expanding air exerts lower pressure while the cold, more dense air found at the Poles exerts higher pressure. The atmosphere is constantly trying to bring these varying pressures back into balance or into a state of equilibrium.

In an enclosed system where the volume remains constant (like a jar or tire), there is a direct relationship between temperature and pressure: as temperature increases, pressure increases. However, in the vast ocean of air called the atmosphere, the relationship of temperature and pressure is much more complex and the two cannot always be equated.

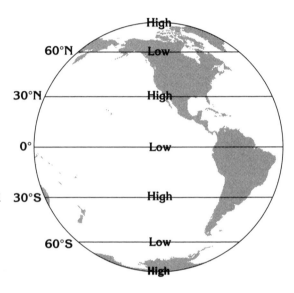

General air pressure patterns

Teaching about Air

Children can grasp most easily those things that are tangible. Air is, at best, a difficult subject in which to delve because it is generally invisible. Like all kinds of matter, it is made of molecules, entities too small to be seen. And yet we are attempting to understand how this matter behaves, what properties it has. It may all seem a bit magical to upper elementary students.

Why even tackle the topic of air pressure at this level? In spite of the difficulties, air pressure remains one of the key elements of weather. It is hard to ignore. The multiple observations students are asked to make capitalize on their curiosity and help them build a repertoire of experiences. The emphasis is on the qualitative, not the quantitative. By having students observe the effects of air on things and how pressure differences cause changes in weather, we hope to feed their excitement about science and to enrich their idea of how the world works.

Learning is a journey, not a destination; we never reach the point at which everything has been learned. Talk to your students. Learn how they are interpreting what they see, how the concepts are forming in their minds. They are on a journey that will last a lifetime.

The Troposphere

Weather takes place in the troposphere, the layer of air closest to Earth. This layer varies from about 8 kilometers (5 miles) thick over the Poles to about 19 kilometers (12 miles) thick over the Equator. On a 16-inch globe, the troposphere would only be as thick as a coat of paint.

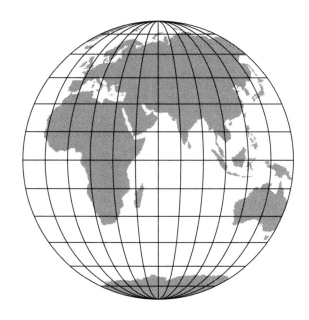

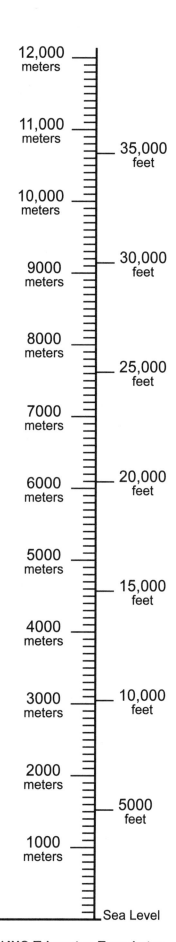

Compare the altitudes of these objects in the troposphere by drawing them beside the scale.

Rising from sea level...

Tallest building (Kuala Lumpur)	452 m
Mt. McKinley (Alaska)	6194 m
Mt. Everest (Nepal)	8848 m

In the air...

Stratus clouds	about 2000 m
Cirrus clouds	about 8000 m
Passenger jets	10,000 m

Interesting fact: The altitude of the International Space Station is about 370,000 m (370km), well above the troposphere.

Air Pressure Proverbs

Proverbs are short, common-sense sayings based on people's observations. Which ones do you think are accurate predictors of weather? Design an investigation to test one of the proverbs.

Wind, Rain, and Snow

When the glass (*barometer*) falls low,
Prepare for a blow;
When the glass is high,
Let your kites fly.

In the winter, a heavy snow is predicted if the barometer falls and the temperature rises.

People Behavior

When the barometer's low,
Teachers say that children misbehave more.

People work better, eat more, and sleep more soundly when the barometer is high.

Birds of a Feather

If the goose flies high, fair weather;
If the goose flies low, foul weather.

Birds flying low,
Expect rain and a blow.

Dogs

If dogs howl, expect a storm.

Trees

Sap from the maple tree flows faster before a rain shower.

Aches and Pains

If your corns all ache and itch,
The weather fair will make a switch.

When your joints all start to ache,
Rainy weather is at stake.

Air Pressure Proverbs

Teacher Notes

"The trouble with weather proverbs is not so much that they're all wrong, but that they're not all right for all times in all places."

NOAA reprint of "Weather Proverbs" by R.E. Spencer (1979)

Wind, Rain, and Snow

When the glass falls low,
Prepare for a blow;
When the glass is high,
Let your kites fly.

In the winter, a heavy snow is predicted if the barometer falls and the temperature rises.

Comments

A falling barometer indicates a storm is likely while a rising barometer is a sign of fair weather.

Trees

Sap from the maple tree flows faster before a rain shower.

A falling barometer, which often indicates a coming storm, allows sap to move faster because of the greater relative pressure differences between the sap and the reduced outside air pressure.

Dogs

If dogs howl, expect a storm.

When the barometer falls, absorbed gases escape body fluids and settle as small bubbles in body tissues, causing irritation in animals—and people.

Birds

If the goose flies high, fair weather;
If the goose flies low, foul weather.

Birds flying low,
Expect rain and a blow.

It has been observed that many birds fly low or do not fly at all before a storm. Geese, for instance, adjust their flight according to optimum air density, higher in the sky during high pressure (fair weather) and closer to the ground during low pressure (foul weather). It is harder to fly in less-dense, low-pressure air.

People Behavior

When the barometer's low,
Teachers say that children misbehave more.

People work better, eat more, and sleep more soundly when the barometer is high.

A study in Wisconsin (1964) indicated low pressure was associated with poor conduct among students. What do you observe?

Aches and Pains

If your corns all ache and itch,
The weather fair will make a switch.

When your joints all start to ache,
Rainy weather is at stake.

As the air pressure falls, the tissues of the body swell. This intensifies the pain of arthritis, a bad tooth, corns, and/or old injuries.

Air Pockets

Topic
Properties of air: takes up space

Key Question
How can we determine if air takes up space?

Focus
By doing a variety of short investigations, students will observe that air takes up space.

Guiding Documents
Project 2061 Benchmarks
- *Air is a substance that surrounds us, takes up space, and whose movement we feel as wind.*
- *Offer reasons for their findings and consider reasons suggested by others.*
- *Make sketches to aid in explaining procedures or ideas.*

NRC Standards
- *Employ simple equipment and tools to gather data and extend the senses.*
- *Scientists develop explanations using observations (evidence) and what they already know about the world (scientific knowledge). Good explanations are based on evidence from investigations.*
- *Earth materials are solid rocks and soils, water, and the gases of the atmosphere. The varied materials have different physical and chemical properties, which make them useful in different ways, for example, as building materials, as sources of fuel, or for growing the plants we use as food. Earth materials provide many of the resources that humans use.*

Science
Physical science
matter

Integrated Processes
Observing
Predicting
Collecting and recording data
Comparing and contrasting
Interpreting data

Materials
For each group:
plastic bag
wide-mouthed transparent jar
rubber band or string
2 two-liter transparent bottles
connector (see *Management 1*)
funnel
clay
plastic tub or other water container
2 transparent cups, 8- or 10-oz.
piece of Styrofoam™
water
paper towels or hand towels

Background Information
Matter may take the form of a gas, a liquid, or a solid. Air is matter. Students may not think air is real because it is invisible. This makes it less tangible and more of a challenge to address. While studying air, it is possible for students to think that some kind of magic is causing things to happen. We can begin to dispel this thinking through multiple experiences that require careful and thoughtful observation.

Air takes up space. Spaces we think of as being empty are almost always filled with air. In order for another substance to fill these spaces, the air must be removed. If air cannot escape, other matter simply cannot move into that space. The bag resists being pushed into the jar (1), the water in the inverted bottle (2) and funnel (3) does not flow downward, and water does not enter the inverted cup (4) because air is already occupying those spaces; there is no room for any other matter.

When air can escape or be moved, space is made for water to enter. Air cannot escape the closed system in *Air Pockets 2* but it can be pushed into the water bottle, allowing water to flow into the air bottle. A hole in the clay seal (3) or a tilt of the inverted cup (4) lets air out and allows water in.

Management
1. It is important to use sturdy plastic bags without leaks. Transparent jars, bottles, and cups are necessary so students can see what is happening. Connectors, sometimes called tornado tubes, can be found at toy stores.

   Instead of connectors, a temporary sealed system can be made with cardboard, clay, and duct tape. Cut a cardboard circle, the diameter of the bottle opening, and punch a $\frac{1}{4}$- to $\frac{3}{8}$-inch hole in the center. Partially fill one of the bottles with water, put the cardboard on the rim, and invert the other bottle over it. Seal with a generous clay collar, topped with a layer of duct tape. Take care that the bottles are vertically aligned and the seal is tight.

2. The activities are intended for small groups of two or three.
3. If groups rotate through activity stations, fewer materials will be needed. Think about having two or more sets of stations. The materials may be grouped at each station beforehand or centrally located for students to gather.
4. Since students will be using water, consider a sink or a plastic tub to catch spills or go outdoors. Towels will help with cleanup.

Procedure
1. Encourage students to share what they know about air. As they study the properties of air today and in other activities, use these ideas to expand their knowledge as well as to help dispel naive conceptions.
2. Tell students they will be using their sense of sight today to learn about air.
3. Give students the task cards and read through the instructions for each part. Demonstrate the setup, if needed, but do not do the activity in front of the class. (It may take some work to make the clay seal airtight in *Air Pockets 3*.)
4. Remind students to read the instructions again before performing each activity, then write their predictions and record their observations.
5. Explain the rotation system or other means of organization for doing the activities. Direct groups to the needed materials.
6. Have students complete the four investigations.
7. Hold a culminating discussion.

Discussion
Air Pockets 1
1. What did you predict would happen?
2. What did you observe? [The bag would not go into the jar.] Were you surprised? Why do you think this happened? [Air was already in the jar so there was no space for the bag.]
3. How did it feel when you pushed against the plastic bag? [Hard, like the air was pushing back.]
4. What do you think would have to happen in order for the bag to go into the jar? [Some of the air would have to escape.] Try it.

Air Pockets 2
1. What did you predict would happen?
2. What did you observe? [The water, in spite of gravity, stayed in the top bottle.] Why do you think this

happened? [The air took up the space in the bottom bottle so there was no room for the water.]
3. How did you make water flow into the other bottle? [Squeeze the water bottle and you will see bubbles of air being pushed into the water bottle, making room for water in the air bottle. Or hold the bottle apparatus parallel to the floor, allowing air to enter the water bottle and water to enter the air bottle.]

Air Pockets 3
1. What was your prediction?
2. What happened? [The water did not go into the bottle.]
3. How might you explain this? [Air filled the bottle and had no way to escape, so there was no room for the water.]
4. How could you get water to flow into the bottle? [make a hole in the clay so air can escape]

Air Pockets 4
1. What did you predict would happen? How did your earlier experiences affect your prediction?
2. What did you observe? [The cup did not fill with water and the Styrofoam™ went down with it.]
3. Why do you think this happened? [There was air in the cup when it was put under water. As long as the air couldn't escape, there was no room for the water to come in. Air takes up space.]
4. How did you move the air from one cup to the other? [Tilt the air-filled cup under the cup filled with water. As bubbles of air entered the water cup, some water was pushed out to make space for the air.] What happened to each cup as you did that? [The air cup took in more water, raising its water level and the water cup took in more air, lowering its water level.]

Culmination
1. From all of these experiences, what did we learn about air? [Air takes up space. Air is real even though it is invisible.]
2. What examples from real life show that no two things can occupy the same space at the same time. [One example: Inflated car air bags occupy the space between the person and the steering wheel or dashboard. The person cannot be in the same space at the same time as the air bags.]

* Reprinted with permission from *Principles and Standards for School Mathematics,* 2000 by the National Council of Teachers of Mathematics. All rights reserved.

Connections
Weather takes place in the troposphere, the layer of air nearest the Earth. An understanding of weather is partially dependent on a knowledge of the properties of air. Though air is composed mostly of invisible gases, it—like all forms of matter—does have properties that can be observed. In this series of investigations, we learned that air takes up space. As long as air remains in a space, no other matter can occupy the same space.
Air also has weight, a property that will be observed in the next activity, *Air Aware.*

Air Pockets 1

Materials
Plastic bag
Wide-mouthed transparent jar
Rubber band or string

Prediction

Observations

What you'll do:
Put the fully-opened bag over the jar and tightly seal with a rubber band or string. Gently push the bag into the jar with a fist.

Air Pockets 2

Materials
2 2-L transparent bottles
Connector
Water

Prediction

Observations

What you'll do:
Fill one bottle with water and attach the connector. Turn the other bottle upside-down and attach it to the connector. Quickly flip the bottles so that the one with water is on top.

Find a way to make water flow into the other bottle. Explain.

Air Pockets 3

Materials
Funnel
2-L transparent bottle
Water
Clay

What you'll do:
Set the funnel in a jar and tightly seal the neck of the jar to the funnel with clay. Pour water into it.

Prediction

Observations

Air Pockets 4

Materials
Plastic tub
2 transparent cups
Piece of Styrofoam™
Water

What you'll do:
Float a piece of Styrofoam™ in a container about half-filled with water. Turn a cup upside-down over the Styrofoam™ and push straight down.

Prediction

Observations

Fill a second cup with water. Find a way to transfer air from the first cup to the second cup while keeping both cups underwater. Sketch or describe what you did.

Topic
Properties of air: has weight

Key Question
How can we determine if air has weight?

Focus
Students will observe that air has weight by constructing a balloon balance and releasing the compressed air from one of the balloons.

Guiding Documents
Project 2061 Benchmarks
- *Air is a substance that surrounds us, takes up space, and whose movement we feel as wind.*
- *Make sketches to aid in explaining procedures or ideas.*

NRC Standards
- *Employ simple equipment and tools to gather data and extend the senses.*
- *Use data to construct a reasonable explanation.*

NCTM Standards 2000*
- *Understand such attributes as length, area, weight, volume, and size of angle and select the appropriate type of unit for measuring each attribute*
- *Collect data using observations, surveys, and experiments*

Math
Equalities and inequalities
    equal to, greater than, less than

Science
Physical science
    matter

Integrated Processes
Observing
Predicting
Collecting and recording data
Comparing and contrasting
Interpreting data

Materials
For each group:
    pencil
    masking tape
    2 straws
    2 safety pins, medium or large
    2 paper clips, regular
    2 pieces of thread, about 30 cm each
    2 9-inch balloons

Background Information
Air is invisible but its properties are observable. In this activity the students will discover that air has weight. At standard pressure at sea level (1013 millibars or 30 inches of mercury) and a temperature of 20°C (68°F), one liter of air weighs 1.2 grams.[1]

Although, technically, a balance is used to determine mass, in this activity the balance is being used to show weight comparison. Its purpose is to compare weight, not to measure specific quantities. The straw balance is sensitive to small differences and is easy to construct. The balance, with the inflated balloons in place, is first equalized; its arm should be parallel to the floor or a table. Any change in the angle of the arm indicates that one side has become heavier (greater than) or lighter (less than).

Although exhaled air rather than atmospheric air is used in this activity, it has minimal effect on the results. This is because the weight of exhaled air is not significantly different from the weight of atmospheric air, particularly with the small volume of air being observed and with a tool that is only meant to show relative comparisons.

Why not use atmospheric air? Air cannot be weighed in air, unless it is compressed, just as water cannot be weighed in water. If the balloons in this activity were replaced by two plastic bags of atmospheric air, no change would occur in the angle of the arm because the air pressure outside the bag would equal the air pressure inside the bag. If air is compressed, as with the inflated balloons, the greater air pressure inside the balloon compared to the pressure outside the balloon allows for change.

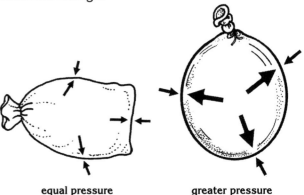

equal pressure   greater pressure

1. Gardner, Robert. *Science Project Ideas About Air.* Enslow Publishers, Inc. Springfield, NJ. 1997.

Management

1. Make a sample balance beforehand so you understand how it is constructed. Widen the hole in the straw until the balance moves freely. The open paper clips should fit snugly over the straws.
2. Divide the class into several groups, each of which should construct and use a balance. Smaller groups are best.
3. The two balloons should be inflated to approximately the same size.
4. Caution students to be careful with the safety pins. The first pin will form the pivot on the balance. The second pin will be used to puncture the balloon near the neck so it releases air slowly instead of popping.
5. Be aware that it takes some time for the air to exit the punctured balloon. However, change can usually be noticed within the first ten minutes.
6. Because the balloon balance is sensitive to air currents, advise students to keep their own motions to a minimum.
7. If students have not previously brainstormed what they know about air, do so before starting this activity. Refer to their comments when appropriate.

Procedure

1. Hold a book (or another object) in your hand. Ask, "Does this book weigh anything?" [Yes.] "How do you know?" [It feels heavy when you hold it.] "What about air? Do you think air has weight?" Have several students take turns holding the book in one hand and an inflated balloon in the other hand. Elicit their comments. Explain that today they are going to observe whether air has weight.
2. Have materials available for each group to gather. Direct groups to construct and equalize their balances, following the directions on the activity page. Have them note that the balance can be described with an equal sign.
3. Instruct students to predict what will happen when they slowly let air out of one balloon. Explain that this can be done in either of two ways: a) put a piece of tape on the stretched balloon and poke with a safety pin, or b) puncture the balloon near the neck, where the skin is not stretched much and is a more solid color.

4. Have groups puncture the balloon, being careful not to disturb the position of the paper clips, and observe the results. Change can usually be observed within the first ten minutes. Several punctures may be made to help this process. You can feel the air being released by holding your hand near the punctures.
5. Direct students to draw a picture of the balloons and balance after the compressed air from one balloon has been released. Have them use an =, <, or > sign to describe the balance.
6. Conduct a class discussion after which students should write what they have discovered.

Discussion

1. What did you observe as the compressed air was leaving the balloon? [The balance slowly went down on the untouched balloon's side or up on the leaky balloon's side.]
2. What did you discover? [Air weighs something.]
3. How is the balloon balance like a seesaw? [When the weights on each end are equal, the seesaw and balloon balance are parallel to the ground. When one side weighs more than the other, the heavier side goes down.]
4. How much would you estimate the air in the balloon weighs? [less than a gram (see *Extension*)]

Extension

Determine the weight of the air in the inflated balloon by hanging a piece of string on the paper clip with the deflated balloon. Cut pieces from the string until the balance equalizes. This remaining length of string represents the weight of the air that was in the balloon. Hold the piece of string in one hand and something weighing one gram in the other hand or put the string and gram on opposite sides of a pan balance. How would you describe the weight of the string? [lighter than one gram]

* Reprinted with permission from *Principles and Standards for School Mathematics*, 2000 by the National Council of Teachers of Mathematics. All rights reserved.

Connections

The medium of weather is the atmosphere, air. Though mostly invisible, this composition of gases does have weight, as was proved in this activity. This is crucial to the study of weather because any kind of matter must have weight in order to exert pressure. No weight, no pressure. Air pressure is one of the four key elements of weather, a property that will be experienced next in *Pressure Points*.

AIR AWARE

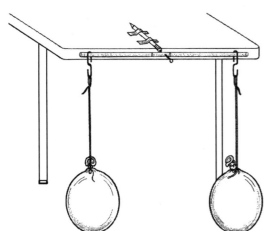

Materials
Pencil	2 paper clips
Masking tape	2 pieces of thread
2 straws	2 9-inch balloons
2 safety pins	

Building the balance
1. Tape the pencil so that the eraser hangs over the end of a table.
2. Squish the end of one straw and push about 2 cm into the other straw. Insert a safety pin through the center of the double straw and firmly into the pencil eraser. Widen the hole until the straw balance moves freely.
3. Place an open paper clip about 1 cm from each end of the double straw.
4. Inflate both balloons to about the same size and knot. Use thread to hang one balloon on each paper clip.
5. Slide the paper clips until the balloons are balanced.

What do you predict will happen when you let the air out of one balloon?

Draw and write what did happen. Use =, <, or > to describe the balance.

What did you discover?

PRESSURE POINTS

Topic
Properties of air: pressure

Key Questions
1. How does pressure feel?
2. What evidence shows air is pressing on the Earth?

Focus
Students will feel the pressure of the air and observe its effects by performing several investigations.

Guiding Documents
Project 2061 Benchmarks
- *Air is a substance that surrounds us, takes up space, and whose movement we feel as wind.*
- *Scientists' explanations about what happens in the world come partly from what they observe, partly from what they think. Sometimes scientists have different explanations for the same set of observations. That usually leads to their making more observations to resolve the differences.*

NRC Standards
- *Employ simple equipment and tools to gather data and extend the senses.*
- *Communicate investigations and explanations.*
- *Scientists develop explanations using observations (evidence) and what they already know about the world (scientific knowledge). Good explanations are based on evidence from investigations.*
- *Earth materials are solid rocks and soils, water, and the gases of the atmosphere. The varied materials have different physical and chemical properties, which make them useful in different ways, for example, as building materials, as sources of fuel, or for growing the plants we use as food. Earth materials provide many of the resources that humans use.*

Science
Physical science
    matter
    force and motion

Integrated Processes
Observing
Predicting
Collecting and recording data
Comparing and contrasting
Interpreting data

Materials
For each group:
    3 plastic bags
    3 straws
    string
    tape
    book
    bicycle pump, preferably with a gauge
    bicycle tire or basketball
    plastic bottle with cap
    water
    pushpin or nail
    2 cups
    2 rings made from 4 cm x 30 cm tagboard strips
    newspaper, half-sheet

Background Information
    Air has weight; it must have weight to exert pressure. Air pressure is defined as the weight of air per unit area. At sea level, the air presses on the Earth with a force of 10 newtons (a metric weight measure equivalent to about 2.2 pounds) per square centimeter or 14.7 pounds per square inch. At sea level, that force is roughly equivalent to the weight of 10 cars (22,000 pounds) pressing on one square meter! As you climb further and further above sea level, the air is less dense so there is less pressure than at sea level. In Denver, the mile-high city, the air pressure is 85% of that at sea level.

    Air pressure is the impact of air molecules colliding with each other and whatever they touch. We do not sense the pressure of the air because 1) the motion of the air molecules occurs in every direction—up, down, front, back, and every angle in between—and 2) the tissues, fluids, and air within our bodies are pressing back against the outside air.

    In the first part of this activity, *Feeling Pressure,* students use their sense of touch to experience pressure, in various forms, qualitatively. When matter is in a state of equilibrium, the physical environment is in balance. This is simulated by two students pressing their hands against each other with equal force; they remain in the same position.

But people have found it useful to create unequal forces to serve specific purposes. *Book Bag* and *Pump It Up* demonstrate that compressed air, which has a higher pressure than the atmosphere, can support weight. When air in a bag is compressed by the weight of the book, the increased pressure inside the bag holds it up. The air pumped into car tires, usually to a pressure of 30-35 pounds per square inch (psi), must be greater than the pressure of the surrounding air (14.7 psi) in order to support the car. A balloon or soap bubble would not fill and expand unless the compressed air had greater pressure to push against the tension of its stretchy skin as well as the outside air.

If there is higher pressure outside than inside a container, it is forceful enough to keep water from streaming out a hole in a bottle (*There's a Hole in My Bucket*) or dropping from a straw (*Straw Transport*). In these activities an airtight system shuts off the weight of the outside air, causing the air pressure inside the system to be less than the air pressure outside the system.

Unequal pressures are also at work in *Paper Lift*. There is very little air under a flat newspaper so the greater air pressure pushing down on it is strong enough to keep the newspaper from being lifted.

Of the properties of air, pressure is one of the most difficult to understand. Since air is invisible and its pressure is not normally felt, it is hard for children to believe it presses on us, that it is a force. Even when children do these activities, they may find it hard to believe that air pressure is the cause of what they observe. By giving students multiple experiences, it is hoped they will begin to see evidence of air pressure at work and realize that it is real.

Management

1. Predictions are encouraged for several of the activities, particularly *Book Bag*, *There's a Hole in My Bucket*, and *Paper Lift*.
2. *Back and Forth*, *Book Bag*, and *There's a Hole in My Bucket* require an airtight system. Students may need to work at making successful seals.
3. Activities involving water are best done over a sink, over a plastic tub, or outdoors.
4. The whole class may move through the activities together (as done in *Procedure*) or students can rotate through stations. There is a deliberate order to the activities so it is recommended that the order not be changed.

Procedure

Feeling Pressure
1. Distribute *Part One* and have students pair off with someone nearly the same size. Review the instructions for *People Press*, have pairs try the experience as well as the *Challenge,* and record their results.
2. Direct students to do *In Your Face.*
3. Instruct student pairs to assemble the straw/plastic bag apparatus for *Back and Forth*. Stress that the system must be airtight.
4. Have students do *Back and Forth* and record the sensations they felt.
5. Challenge (optional): Remove one plastic bag from the double straw. Fill the other bag with air. Press on the bag to move a foam peanut across a smooth surface. Race with others. What method of pushing air moved the peanut the farthest? Which method helped you best control the peanut's movement?
6. Discuss the activities on the first page.

Observing Pressure
1. Give students the *Observing Pressure* pages. Have them predict what will happen when they do *Book Bag* and then record what happens.
2. Monitor as students take turns pumping up a tire or ball (and, if there is one, reading the pressure gauge) suggested in *Pump It Up*.
3. Instruct students to read the directions for *There's a Hole in My Bucket*, predict what will happen in each of the two experiences, try it, and record the results.
4. Have students find and record a way to transfer water using a straw in *Straw Transport*.
5. Direct students to read the instructions for *Paper Lift*, predict what will happen, perform the investigations, and record the results.
6. Discuss the activities on these two pages.

Discussion

Feeling Pressure
1. How did equal pressure feel? How did unequal pressure feel?
2. Air pressure pushes at you from all directions. How does it feel? [You don't notice it.] How does that relate to what you felt in *People Press?* [It's like when both of us were pressing with the same force. You don't feel the pressure; you're balanced.]
3. Did you feel the air move when you pressed your cheek (*In Your Face*)? ... when you pressed the plastic bag (*Back and Forth*)? How would you describe that feeling?

Observing Pressure

Book Bag

1. What did you learn about air? [Air can lift things or hold things up.]

Pump It Up

1. (if a pressure gauge were used) How did the strength you needed to pump relate to the pressure gauge reading? [The higher the pressure, the more difficult it was to pump.]
2. Name some ways compressed air is used to support weight. [in tires which hold up cars and bicycles, bounce houses, air mattresses, etc.]

There's a Hole in My Bucket

1. What happened when the cap was off? [The water came out of the hole.]
2. Where was the air pressing? [The air was pressing equally against the top of the bottle and against the hole.]
3. How might this explain what happened? [With air pressure being equal in all directions, the pressure of the water was stronger and the water came out.]
4. What happened when the cap was in place? [The water stayed in the bottle.]
5. Where was the air pressing? [The weight of the air was cut off at the top of the bottle so there was greater air pressure against the hole, strong enough pressure to keep the water inside the bottle.]

Straw Transport

1. How did you use the straw to move the water? [immerse the straw in water, put a finger over the straw, move the straw to the other cup, and lift the finger]
2. Where was the air pressing when the finger blocked the top of the straw? [The pressure pushing against the bottom of the straw was strong enough to keep the water in the straw.]
3. Where was air pressing when the finger was lifted? [It was pressing equally down through the top of the straw as well as up through the bottom of the straw. With the air pressure being equal, the pressure of the water caused it to spill.]

Paper Lift

1. With the tagboard rings in place, where was the air pressing? [It was pressing equally on all sides of the paper. The speed of the lift did not change this so the force of the lift overcame the equalized air pressure and raised the newspaper.]
2. With the newspaper flat against the surface, where is the air pressing? [down against the paper]
3. Why did the newspaper come up when the string was pulled slowly? [There was time for the air to rush underneath the paper and press up, down, and in all directions.]
4. What happened when the string was pulled rapidly? [It broke through the tape, leaving the newspaper behind.] How can this be explained? [There was not time for air to enter under the paper so the greater air pressure pushing down on the paper caused it to stay put.]

 Journal prompt: Imagine you met someone that didn't believe air existed because it is invisible. Describe how you would try to convince this person that air really does exist.

Extension

To expand upon the concept of air pressure with capable students, do the activity, *Look Out Below!* found in the AIMS publication *Spills and Ripples*. It deals with an inverted glass of water.

Home Link

With the guidance of an adult family member, encourage students to use a gauge to measure the air pressure in their cars' tires. Have them talk to adults about recommended tire pressures and what happens when the air pressure gets too low. [affects gas mileage, car rides differently, etc.]

* Reprinted with permission from *Principles and Standards for School Mathematics*, 2000 by the National Council of Teachers of Mathematics. All rights reserved.

Connections

Since weather takes place within the Earth's atmosphere, the pressure of the air is an important influence. The unequal heating of the Earth causes temperature variations which, in turn, cause differences in air pressure. Warm air expands, lowering the air pressure, while cool air is more dense and exerts higher pressure.

Now that we have established some evidence that air pressure exists, the next step is to measure it. *High and Lows* offers a simple homemade barometer from which general air pressure trends—rising, falling, steady—can be noted.

PRESSURE POINTS

Feeling Pressure

People Press

Stand, facing another person, a small distance apart.
With arms outstretched, press your palms together.
Press against each other with equal force.
What happens?

Now have one person press with less force than the other.
What happens?

Challenge: Sit on the floor with your backs against each other and legs in front of you. Lock elbows and press against each other to get to a standing position. Which works best, equal or unequal force?

In Your Face

Puff out your cheek on one side. While keeping your mouth closed, press against your cheek. Then move the air from one cheek to the other. What do you feel?

Back and Forth

Insert one straw about 2 cm into the other straw and seal the seam with tape. Attach a plastic bag to each end of the double straw by wrapping tightly with layers of string and sealing with tape. Each bag should be more than half-filled with air. Push air from one bag to the other. How does it feel?

Materials
2 plastic bags
2 straws
String
Tape

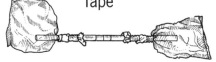

PRESSURE POINTS

Materials
Plastic bag
String
Tape
Book

Book Bag
Gather a plastic bag around the end of a straw and wrap tightly with several layers of string. Put tape over the string. Place a book on the bag and blow through the straw. What happens?

What does this tell you about air?

Pump It Up
Use a pump to add air to a bicycle tire or inflate a basketball. Watch the pressure gauge. How does pumping the air feel?

Materials
Bicycle pump
Bicycle tire or basketball

There's a Hole in My Bucket
Poke a hole near the bottom of the plastic bottle. In a sink or over a plastic tub, fill the bottle with water. What happens?

Materials
Plastic bottle with cap
Water
Pushpin or nail

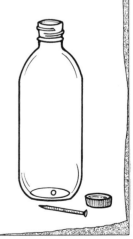

Now fill the bottle with water and seal with the cap. What happens?

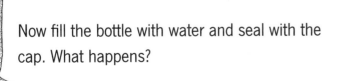

PRESSURE POINTS

Straw Transport

Set two cups on a table. Move water from one cup to the other using only a straw. The straw may not touch your mouth.

Describe your solution.

Materials
2 cups, one with water
Straw

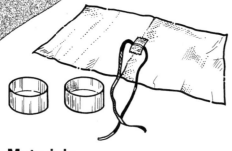

Paper Lift

Tape the center of the string to the center of the newspaper. Place the two rings about 15 cm apart and lay the newspaper over them. Hold the ends of the string and raise it slowly. Put the newspaper back in place over the rings and pull the string rapidly. What happens?

Materials
Newspaper, half-sheet
Transparent tape
String
2 rings (from 4 cm x 30 cm
    tagboard strips)

Now remove the rings and lay the newspaper flat on the table. Raise the string slowly. Repeat, raising the string rapidly. What happens?

Topic
Weather station: balloon barometer

Key Question
How can changes in air pressure be measured?

Focus
Students will construct a simple barometer and use it to track air pressure patterns over time.

Guiding Documents
Project 2061 Benchmarks
- *Air is a substance that surrounds us, takes up space, and whose movement we feel as wind.*
- *Things change in steady, repetitive, or irregular ways—or sometimes in more than one way at the same time. Often the best way to tell which kinds of change are happening is to make a table or graph of measurements.*
- *Make sketches to aid in explaining procedures or ideas.*
- *Recognize when comparisons might not be fair because some conditions are not kept the same.*

NRC Standards
- *Employ simple equipment and tools to gather data and extend the senses.*
- *Weather changes from day to day and over the seasons. Weather can be described by measurable quantities, such as temperature, wind direction and speed, and precipitation.*

NCTM Standards 2000*
- *Select and use benchmarks to estimate measurements*
- *Collect data using observations, surveys, and experiments*

Math
Measurement
   reading a scale
Equalities and inequalities
   greater than, less than, equal to
Decimals

Science
Earth science
   meteorology
Physical science
   properties of air

Integrated Processes
Observing
Collecting and recording data
Comparing and contrasting
Controlling variables
Interpreting data
Relating

Materials
Pint jar
9" round balloon
Large rubber band
Glue
Straw, cut in half
Tape

Background Information
Air Pressure

   Air has weight. Air pressure is the weight of air per unit of area. At sea level, air presses with a force of 10 newtons (2.2 pounds) per square centimeter or 14.7 pounds per square inch. Meteorologists measure air or barometric pressure with a barometer and usually report the results in millibars.

   Temperature affects air pressure, but this is a complex relationship dependent on other variables. For this reason, warm air may have high or low pressure. The same is true of cold air.

   Air pressure also changes with elevation. Standard pressure at sea level is 1013 millibars (29.92 inches of mercury). The higher the elevation, the lower the air pressure.

   There are normal daily pressure patterns, in which the pressure changes are slow. However, quick drops or rises in pressure are an important indicator of weather changes. Lowering pressure generally means cooler or stormy weather is coming. Rising pressure most often results in fair, sunny days.

Balloon Barometer

The balloon barometer is, at best, an inexact tool for measuring air pressure. It can easily measure temperature rather than air pressure unless it is placed in a location where the temperature remains relatively constant. Why? Temperature changes cause air pressure changes *inside the jar* because the air is trapped in a contained space. Warm, expanding air, having no place to escape, exerts higher pressure and colder air exerts lower pressure. To reflect the atmospheric pressure *outside the jar,* the variable being measured, the pressure inside the jar needs to be controlled.

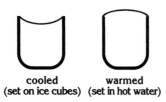

cooled   warmed
(set on ice cubes)   (set in hot water)

These temperature conditions show pressure changes inside the jar, *not* the atmospheric pressure outside the jar.

The advantages of the balloon barometer are that it is inexpensive, simple to make, and can show general changes in air pressure. The emphasis is on observing change and how air pressure change results in certain kinds of weather. This is worthy and realistic goal for children at this stage of development.

If the temperature is kept fairly constant, the balloon barometer measures the air pressing from outside of the jar. When first constructed, the air pressure is equal inside and outside the jar. The balloon skin is level or flat. This is a benchmark measurement so it should be done at a time when the air pressure is normal for your area.

High pressure exists when the outside air pressure is greater than the pressure inside the jar. If the outside air pressure is high, it presses against the balloon skin with more force than the air that is pressing inside the jar; the skin forms a depression. *Low pressure exists when the outside air pressure is less than the pressure inside the jar.* If the outside air pressure is low, the greater air pressure inside the jar causes the skin to bulge outward.

Low pressure   Normal pressure   High pressure

Management

1. Previous work with air pressure (see *Pressure Points*) is important for understanding.
2. When constructing the barometer, choose a day with normal air pressure for your area because all the readings will be relative to the pressure that day. To find your area's normal air pressure, call the nearest National Weather Service station.
3. The numbers on the barometer scale are only for making comparisons and do not represent any customary unit of measurement used by meteorologists. Record simply as 5.4, for example. The scale may be laminated so students can mark the readings from day to day.
4. The barometer responds to temperature changes as well as air pressure changes. In order to measure air pressure, set the barometer in an indoor location where temperature does not vary. (Air pressure is generally the same indoors and outdoors.) Keep a thermometer nearby to monitor how closely temperature is being controlled. Record this temperature each time a barometer reading is taken in order to evaluate its accuracy.
5. If attaching the barometer scale to a wall is a problem, an alternative is to fold a 6" x 9" piece of tagboard lengthwise into 2-inch segments. Form the tagboard into a triangular column along these folds. Stand it next to the barometer and glue the scale so that the straw is pointing to the "5."
6. Over time, the balloon skin will weaken and need to be replaced. As the balloon skin moves in response to the air pressure, the straw may also come loose and need to be re-attached.

Procedure

1. Explain to students that they will be making a tool that can measure air pressure. Give groups the barometer construction page. Have them collect the needed materials and follow the directions. Explain that "5" will represent normal air pressure because the barometer is being constructed on a day with normal air pressure for their area.
2. Ask students to predict how the balloon skin will look during high air pressure and then low air pressure if the temperature is controlled.
3. Distribute the recording page. Instruct students to take regular readings about the same time each day, each time observing changes in the balloon skin, recording the barometer scale number, and noting the kind of weather.

Time: 10:15 A.M.

Date	Barometer	Weather
10-18	5.3	fair
10-19	5.4	sunny
10-20	4.9	cloudy

4. After students have observed the balloon barometer over time, direct them to draw the balloon skin at low, normal, and high pressures (see *Background Information*).
5. Have students begin to relate air pressure changes to weather conditions.
6. Refer back to the *Station Model* activity and add the barometric tendency symbol, indicating change in the past three hours, to the station model.

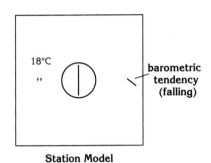

Station Model

Discussion
1. How did the balloon skin look during normal air pressure? [flat] How can this be explained? [The air pressure inside the jar is equal to the air pressure outside the jar.]
2. How did the balloon skin look during low air pressure? [bulged outward] Why? [There is less air pressure pushing down on the balloon from the outside compared to the pressure pushing up from inside the jar. It is the air pressure outside the jar that is being measured.]

3. How did the balloon skin look during high air pressure? [caved inward] Why? [During high pressure, there is greater air pressure pushing from outside the jar than from inside the jar.]
4. What range of air pressure readings did we record over the last two weeks (or whatever length of time the activity was done)? Did it change a small amount or a large amount?
5. If the air pressure is falling, what kind of weather would you predict for tomorrow? [colder, possibly stormy, depending on the strength of the shift]

 Journal prompt: Study your records. How is air pressure related to the kind of weather we have? (To help students see the pattern, have them make two columns labeled *Low* and *High*, respectively, and write their weather descriptions in the appropriate column. With sufficient data, students should conclude that high pressure is related to fair weather and low pressure indicates cooler, maybe stormy weather.)

Extensions
1. Make a line graph of data.
2. Study the highs and lows on a newspaper or computer-generated weather map. Notice how they relate to the position of weather systems.

Connections
The medium of weather is the Earth's atmosphere, so the pressure the air exerts has a direct effect on weather. The changes in air pressure are measured with a barometer. The balloon barometer gives a general idea of air pressure changes, if the temperature is fairly constant.

If you have an aneroid barometer, more precise measurements using customary units can be obtained. Directions and a format for tracking change are found in *Aneroid Barometer.* Air pressure data can also be retrieved from various weather web sites, although this does not involve first-hand data gathering.

After the barometer experiences, students should be assessed on their understanding of the properties of air. A suggestion follows.

HIGHS AND LOWS

Materials
Glass pint jar
9-inch round balloon
Large rubber band
Glue
Straw, cut in half
Tape

Making a Barometer

1. Cut off the neck of the balloon. Stretch the remaining balloon skin tightly over the mouth of the jar and hold it in place with a rubber band.
2. Cut the straw so one end forms a sharp point.
3. Glue the uncut end of the straw from the center to the edge of the balloon. Hold it in place until set.
4. Put the jar and scale in a place where the temperature stays about the same all day. Tape the scale to a wall so that the straw points to the "5."

Barometer Scale

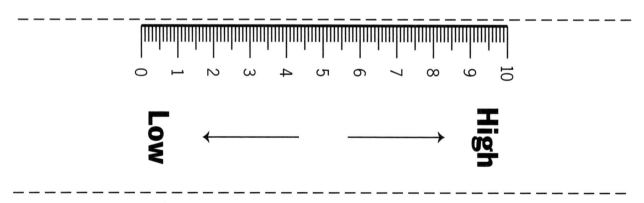

How does air pressure affect the balloon?

Record your barometer readings as well as the weather.

Draw how the balloon skin looks during . . .

U
Low pressure

U
Normal pressure

U
High pressure

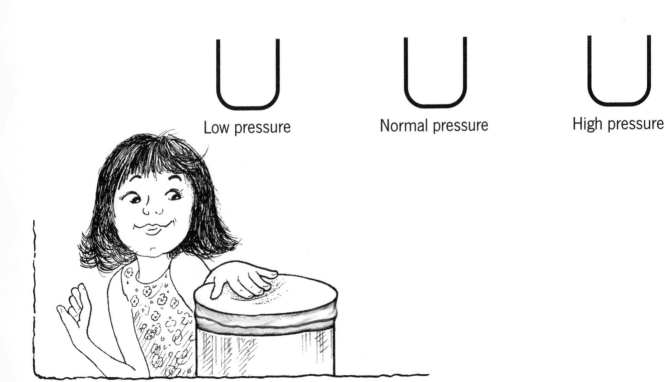

Aneroid Barometer

How can we more precisely measure changes in air pressure?

Changes in air pressure are measured with a barometer. The mercury barometer, invented by Evangelista Torricelli in 1643, has about a 30-inch glass tube filled with mercury. The mercury rises or falls according to the amount of air pressure. In contrast, the aneroid barometer is "without liquid." It has a flexible, accordion-like metal in a tightly sealed chamber from which some of the air has been removed. Air pressure causes the metal to contract or expand, moving a pointer along a scale.

Calibrating the Barometer

With a small screwdriver, turn the central screw at the back of the barometer until the pointer matches the current air pressure data. Weather data are normally reported on an hourly basis and are readily accessible through the various websites listed at the back of this book.

To compare changes in pressure, the second indicator can be manually turned to match the pointer. When the latter changes, before and after measurements can be compared.

Observations of Change

• To introduce students to the aneroid barometer, place it inside the balloon barometer made in *Highs and Lows.*

  For a quick demonstration, have students observe what happens to the pointer as you first depress the balloon skin with your fingers (simulating high pressure) and then pull it outward (simulating low pressure).

  Put the balloon barometer in its normal location and encourage students to note how the aneroid barometer's pointer moves over time as the balloon skin changes in response to weather-related air pressure fluctuations.

• Once students have observed these changes, take the aneroid barometer out of the balloon barometer and place it in an indoor location where the temperature is relatively constant. This will be its permanent home as part of your weather station.

  Changes in barometric pressure can be quite small—a few millibars over the course of a fair day—or quite large when the weather is changing. The next time a front passes through your area, have students track the air pressure measurements at short intervals of time. Dramatic changes in air pressure occur during storms, tornadoes, and similar kinds of weather. A line graph is an appropriate way to show these changes visually. Students can use the next page to record such an event.

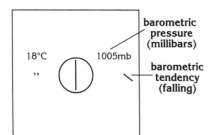

Station Model

Show the barometric pressure measurement in millibars (or inches) on the station model. Data from the aneroid barometer can also be used to determine barometric tendency.

Aneroid Barometer

(title of line graph)

Time

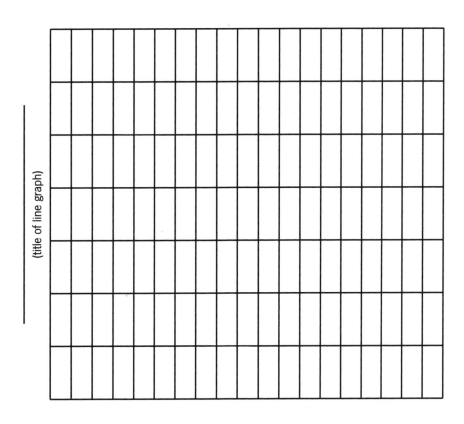

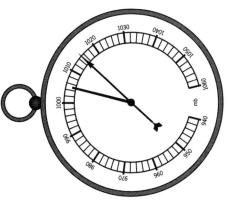

Record air pressure data during noticeable changes in weather.

Time	Air Pressure	Weather

Air Assessment

Essential Question

What are the properties of air?

Learning Goals

- Observe and gather evidence of the properties of air, the medium in which weather exists.
  - Understand that air takes up space.
  - Understand that air has weight.
  - Understand that air exerts pressure, a key component of weather.

Air Assessment

Activity

Write the following on chart paper or a transparency:

> Using objects or illustrations, prove one of these is true. Explain.
>
> **Air takes up space.**
>
> **Air has weight.**
>
> **Air exerts pressure.**

Tell students their proofs must be different from the activities they have recently done. Give students time to collect materials. Consider presentations within small groups 1) to eliminate the copycat effect, 2) to make it less intimidating, and 3) because some properties can be easily shown in only a few ways.

Evidence of Learning

Evaluate the appropriateness of the object in representing the chosen property of air. The use of multiple objects and/or the presentation of a creative picture should be worth extra points.

Listen for a thoughtful explanation that clearly connects the object and the chosen property. Correct scientific language, such as *pressure*, should be used. A student who exceeds expectations might explain how a particular object illustrates more than one property.

Air takes up space.
Objects include packing materials or shoes with air pockets, bubbles, inner tubes or tires, bounce house pictures, air mattresses, rafts, a flattened juice box expanded when air is blown into it, etc. Many of these objects also apply to the pressure property.

Air has weight.
Example: Put an uninflated soccer ball and an inflated soccer ball on opposite sides of a balance. The balance arm leans downward on the side of the inflated ball, showing it weighs more. A student exceeds expectations if he or she goes further by measuring the difference in the weight of the two balls.

Air exerts pressure.
Objects include bubbles, balloons, inner tubes or tires, and air mattresses. The more air is compressed into a given space, the greater its pressure. If the space is enclosed by elastic walls such as the rubber in balloons or the soap film in bubbles, the air pressure causes the walls to bulge outward. Air pressure inside the bubbles, balloons, or tires must be higher than outside air pressure for them to expand.

The Cause of Wind

Due to the tilt of the Earth as it revolves around the sun, this planet is heated unequally. Some locations receive more direct and intense radiation from the sun than others. In addition, land absorbs and emits heat energy more quickly than water. The emission of heat energy from the Earth's surface changes the temperature of the air masses above it.

Variations in the temperature of air masses cause differences in air pressure—and it is air pressure variations that put the air into motion. Winds blow horizontally from high-pressure regions to low-pressure regions in an effort to bring the pressure differences back into balance; nature constantly seeks equilibrium.

Global Forces Affecting Wind

The location and strength of winds are determined by three forces: the pressure gradient force, the Coriolis effect, and friction. *Pressure gradient force* includes two variables: 1) the difference in pressure and 2) the distance between two points. Isobars on surface weather maps show gradients of pressure, changes in pressure per unit distance. The smaller the distance and/or the greater the pressure difference, the stronger the winds. Closely-spaced isobars, most likely found around a low-pressure center, often indicate stormy weather.

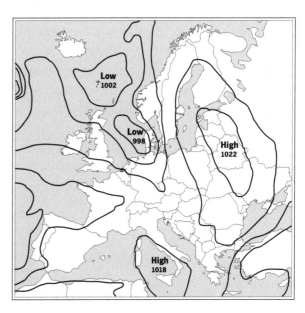

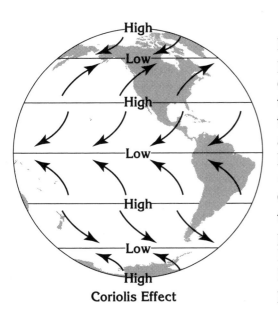

Coriolis Effect

There are recognizable high- and low-pressure bands around the Earth. Since air moves from high-pressure to low-pressure areas, winds would be expected to blow straight north or south. However, the spinning of the Earth causes winds to curve to the right (relative to the direction from which they are coming) in the Northern Hemisphere and to the left in the Southern Hemisphere. This is called the *Coriolis effect*, first identified by Gustave Gaspard de Coriolis (1792-1843) in 1835. The faster the wind, the stronger the effect. It is also why winds in high-pressure systems travel clockwise in the Northern Hemisphere and counterclockwise in the Southern Hemisphere. The opposite is true for winds in low-pressure systems.

As it blows across the Earth's surface, wind is slowed down by *friction*. Friction is least over relatively smooth surfaces such as water, deserts, snow and ice, and plains. But there is greater friction as wind bumps against forests, mountains, and buildings.

Local Wind Systems

Sea breezes occur along oceans, seas, or large lakes, most often in spring and summer when the temperature differences between land and water are greatest. During the day, the land warms more quickly than the water. The cooler, more dense air over water flows toward the warmer, less dense air over land. At night, the land cools more quickly than the water. If there is enough contrast in surface air temperatures, a *land breeze* will start blowing from the land toward the water—from cooler, more dense air to warmer, less dense air.

Sea breeze

Land breeze

Mountains and valleys also generate breezes. During the day, the sun heats the valley. The air begins to rise and is felt as wind along the slopes. These *valley breezes* are most common during the warm season when the sun's radiation is most intense. At night, particularly during the cold season, the cooling, more dense air near the surface of mountain slopes starts a *mountain breeze* flowing downhill toward the warmer, less dense air in the valleys.

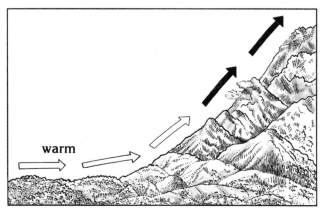

Valley breeze

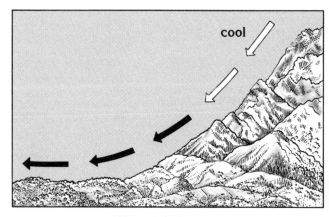

Mountain breeze

Jet Streams

High in the atmosphere, at around 9000 meters (30,000 feet), strong winds develop as a result of significant temperature and pressure differences. These *jet streams* are relatively narrow, 40 to 160 kilometers (25 to 100 miles) wide and two to three kilometers (one to two miles) deep, and form along fronts where cold and warm air masses meet. While jet streams occur in both hemispheres, more is known about the dominant one in the Northern Hemisphere. It generally moves west to east at speeds averaging 184 to 277 kilometers per hour (115 to 173 miles per hour).

During winter, when the temperature and pressure differences intensify, the jet streams are strongest. In the Northern Hemisphere, the polar air pushes the warm-cold boundary southward and the jet stream dips closer to the Equator. During the more uniform temperatures of summer, the jet stream tends to weaken and move toward the Poles.

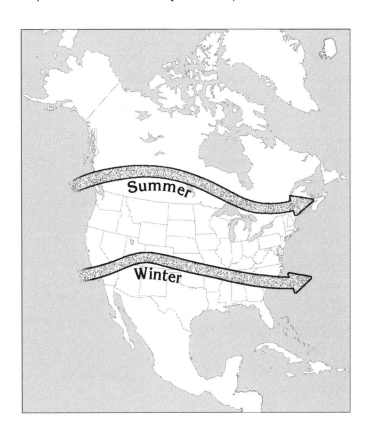

When traveling east at high altitudes, pilots fly in the jet stream to save time and fuel. Jet streams are also important for weather forecasting and predicting the movement of fronts. Because jet streams mark the boundary between warm and cold air, storms tend to track along their paths.

Forecasting

The direction of the wind hints at what kind of weather is coming, whether it will be cooler or warmer, drier or more moist. A gradual shift in wind direction may signal the approach of a front. As the front passes through, the wind may quickly shift 90° or more.

The speed of the wind indicates how fast the weather changes are taking place. A decrease in wind or no wind at all means the present weather will continue. An increase in wind may mean stormy weather is coming. There is also a predictable daily pattern where the wind increases in the afternoon, as the sun's heating causes sharper contrasts in air pressure, and decreases around sunset.

Wind Proverbs

Proverbs are short, common-sense sayings based on people's observations. Which ones do you think are accurate predictors of weather? Design an investigation to test one of the proverbs.

East and West Winds

When the wind is in the west,
The weather is at its best.

When the wind is in the east,
'Tis neither good for man nor beast.

A cow with its tail to the west
Makes weather the best.
A cow with its tail to the east
Makes weather the least.

North and South Winds

A northern air brings weather fair.

When the wind is in the south,
It has rain in its mouth.

Strength of Winds

No weather is ill
If the wind is still.

The winds of the daytime wrestle and fight
Longer and stronger than those of the night.

Sharp horns (crescent moon) do threaten high winds.

Smoke

A storm wind settles in the chimney,
but a clear wind coaxes out the smoke.

Wind Proverbs
Teacher Notes

"The trouble with weather proverbs is not so much that they're all wrong, but that they're not all right for all times in all places."

NOAA reprint of "Weather Proverbs" by R.E. Spencer (1979)

East and West Winds

When the wind is in the west,
The weather is at its best.

When the wind is in the east,
'Tis neither good for man nor beast.

A cow with its tail to the west
Makes weather the best.
A cow with its tail to the east
Makes weather the least.

North and South Winds

A northern air brings weather fair.

When the wind is in the south,
It has rain in its mouth.

Strength of Winds

No weather is ill
If the wind is still.

The winds of the daytime wrestle and fight
Longer and stronger than those of the night.

Sharp horns do threaten high winds.

Smoke

A storm wind settles in the chimney,
but a clear wind coaxes out the smoke.

Comments

Geography determines the reliability of these proverbs. They tend to be truest along the Atlantic coast where east winds blow rain across the land, but not indicative of the Pacific coast where west winds bring rain.

(New England proverb) Animals tend to graze with their backs to the wind, allowing them to detect the scent of enemies coming from behind. Since an east wind brings rain and a west wind brings fair weather in New England, the cow's tail can be a weather sign.

Again, geography determines the truth of these proverbs. Are they true for your location?

When the wind is calm, the weather is likely fair.

Winds generally become stronger in the afternoon, as the sun heats the land and causes sharper temperature/air pressure contrasts between atmosphere and land. The land cools as the sun sets, calming the winds.

The "horns" or ends of a crescent moon are clear (sharp) when there are high winds at upper altitudes. As the winds descend, those winds are felt on Earth.

Weak winds allow smoke to rise and escape; strong winds impede smoke from leaving the chimney.

It's a Breeze!

Topic
Wind direction and speed, informal

Key Question
What do our wind detectors show us about the wind?

Focus
Students will use a ribbon to find wind direction and, from observations, devise a simple wind force scale.

Guiding Documents
Project 2061 Benchmarks
- *Air is a substance that surrounds us, takes up space, and whose movement we feel as wind.*
- *Things change in steady, repetitive, or irregular ways—or sometimes in more than one way at the same time. Often the best way to tell which kinds of change are happening is to make a table or graph of measurements.*
- *Make sketches to aid in explaining procedures or ideas.*

NRC Standards
- *Employ simple equipment and tools to gather data and extend the senses.*
- *Weather changes from day to day and over the seasons. Weather can be described by measurable quantities, such as temperature, wind direction and speed, and precipitation.*
- *The position and motion of objects can be changed by pushing or pulling. The size of the change is related to the strength of the push or pull.*

NCTM Standards 2000*
- *Describe location and movement using common language and geometric vocabulary*
- *Collect data using observations, surveys, and experiments*
- *Use representations to model and interpret physical, social, and mathematical phenomena*

Math
Geometry and measurement
   direction
   change of angle (ribbon)

Science
Earth science
   meteorology

Integrated Processes
Observing
Collecting and recording data
Identifying variables
Comparing and contrasting
Interpreting data
Relating

Materials
For each wind detector:
   60 cm (24") ribbon about 1.5 cm ($\frac{1}{2}$") wide
      (see *Management 1*)
   straw, pencil, or ruler
   tape

For the class:
   several compass roses (see *Management 2*)

Background Information
Wind direction and speed

Wind is moving air. We have wind because of differences in the heating of the Earth which, in turn, causes differences in air pressure. Air moves from areas of high pressure toward areas of low pressure in an attempt to reach equilibrium.

Meteorologists measure both the wind's direction and its speed. Wind direction refers to the direction from which the wind is coming, not where it is going. It is identified using wind vanes and reported as one of the eight directions of a compass (N, NE, E, SE, S, SW, W, NW).

Wind speed is really the strength or force of the wind. The stronger the force, the more effect it will have on sails, trees, cars, tall buildings, etc. It is measured by an anemometer and, in the United States, is usually reported in miles per hour.

Before measuring instruments were invented, people used more qualitative methods to depict the wind. Although wind vanes had been around a long time, anemometers did not exist. It was in 1806 that Sir Francis Beaufort, a ship captain, developed a wind force scale by describing the effects of different strengths of wind on his ship. Later the effects of wind on land were added and, over 100 years later, wind speeds were attached to the numbers on the Beaufort Scale.

To follow the flow of history, students' first observations of the wind should be qualitative, rather than quantitative. Have them look at the effects different strengths of wind have on the surroundings. A ribbon wind detector allows students to "do" science, to determine their own wind force scale. Turn students loose to observe, explore, and look for patterns.

Acquiring a sense of direction

As students become acquainted with using the compass, it is natural for them to begin to relate local landmarks or objects to certain directions. They may notice the yellow house across the street is southeast from their measuring site. Maybe a certain light pole is to the west. Over time, these landmarks may eventually take the place of using a compass rose.

Students may also begin to notice that city streets tend to be laid out in north/south or east/west directions, especially where the land is flat. If there is an airport in town, they may want to observe how the runways are laid out. The direction of the runways relates directly to wind patterns for that area.

Standards for taking wind data

In this activity, students are asked to try their wind detectors in different locations. This will help them become aware that wind direction can differ, even on such a small area as the school grounds. Later, when they use the wind detectors to gather weather station data, the standards meteorologists use become important. Professionals take wind data 10 meters (33 feet) above the ground in an open area. Modified for the school setting, the wind detector should be reasonably high off the ground, say above the shoulders, and away from buildings or large objects.

Management

1. Use a lightweight ribbon such as the satin ribbon often found in fabric and craft stores. Alternatives include strips cut from crepe paper or plastic garbage bags. Ribbons that are too light or too heavy will not show variations in wind strength satisfactorily.
2. To determine wind direction, several compass roses will be needed at the site where wind data will be gathered. If the surface allows, use chalk. If not, draw the compass roses on butcher paper, laminate, and transport outside for readings. Make them large enough so a student can stand in the center.
3. It is simplest to orientate the compass rose by using magnetic north (where the compass points), realizing that the direction will be somewhat of an approximation. Most locations in the continental

United States will not vary more than 20° from geographical north. If you know the declination for your area, found on topographical maps, you can adjust the magnetic compass to geographical north. Another way to determine geographical north is by the layout of the streets. Streets in flat areas tend to be built along north/south and east/west lines.

4. Allow plenty of time for students to observe the effects of the wind both with and without their wind detectors, as suggested in *Part One*. On another day or over a period of time, students can record data gathered from their wind detectors (*Part Two*).

Procedure

Part One: Exploration

1. Go outside and have students observe how the wind affects the flag, trees, dust, etc. How does the flag look? How much are the leaves and branches moving? Is the wind causing the dust to blow?
2. Have students demonstrate being the wind at different strengths. For instance, calm—stand still; light breeze—walk slowly; moderate breeze—jog slowly; and strong breeze—run.
3. Instruct students to tape the ribbon to the end of a straw, pencil, or ruler.
4. Outside, have students observe their wind detector by holding it at different heights, taking it to different places, and using it at different times of the day. Optional: Students might write observations on a piece of scratch paper.
5. Ask students for their observations and record on chart paper. "How did the wind compare at different heights? Did the wind change at different locations? Explain. How did the wind compare at different times of the day? What does your wind detector tell you about the wind? [direction, its relative strength without measuring]
6. Give students the first activity page and have them record their answers to the *Key Question* that was just discussed.
7. As a class, develop a wind force scale. Direct students to label each box and sketch how the ribbon will look in each kind of wind. Suggestion: 0—calm; 1—light breeze; 2—moderate breeze; and 3—strong breeze.

Wind Force Scale

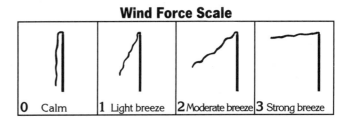

| 0 Calm | 1 Light breeze | 2 Moderate breeze | 3 Strong breeze |

Part Two: Recording wind data

1. Distribute the second activity page and tell students they will now record "official" data gathered from their wind detectors.

2. Take the class outside and have a student stand in a compass rose with the wind detector. Ask, "In which direction is the ribbon blowing? (for example, west).

   Explain that meteorologists report from where the wind is coming which is easily found by facing into the wind. Once students have done that, ask, "From which direction is the wind coming?" (the opposite direction, east in the example).

3. On the activity page, instruct students to record the date and time, draw the ribbon direction on the compass rose, identify from where the wind is coming, and decide which number (or label) on their wind force scale best describes the strength of the wind at that time.

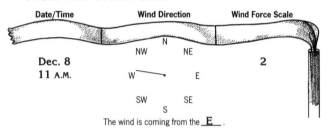

Date/Time — Wind Direction — Wind Force Scale

Dec. 8
11 A.M.

N
NW   NE
W   E
SW   SE
S

2

The wind is coming from the __E__ .

4. Have students gather and record wind data at the same time each day for several days.

5. Discuss their findings.

6. Optional: Have students find the current wind data reported by the media. A student can stand in the middle of a compass rose and become a ribbon wind detector, positioning an arm to demonstrate the reported wind conditions.

7. Relate the qualitative nature of the class wind force scale to the historic *Beaufort Scale* through the pages which follow. Instruct students to cut, order, and glue the numbers (miles per hour) and the pictures, using the descriptions of effects on land, onto the scale.

Beaufort Scale

Number	Description	Mph	Effects on Land	Picture
0	Calm	<1	Smoke rises straight up	
1	Light air	1-3	Smoke drifts; tree leaves barely move; wind vane doesn't move	
2	Light breeze	4-7	Leaves rustle; wind felt on face; wind vane moves	
3	Gentle breeze	8-12	Leaves and twigs move; bits of paper and dust rise from the ground	
4	Moderate breeze	13-18	Small branches move; raises dust and loose paper	
5	Fresh breeze	19-24	Small trees sway	
6	Strong breeze	25-31	Large branches sway; difficult to use umbrellas	
7	Moderate gale (Near gale)	32-38	Whole trees in motion; difficult to walk	
8	Fresh gale	39-46	Twigs break off trees	
9	Strong gale	47-54	Branches break; slight damage to buildings	
10	Whole gale	55-63	Trees blown down; heavy damage to buildings	
11	Storm	64-72	Widespread damage	
12	Hurricane	>72	Extreme damage	

Knots (the original scale measure) or kilometers per hour can be substituted for miles per hour using the comparative values listed in the table. Knots equal 1.15 miles per hour or 1.85 kilometers per hour.

Beaufort Number	Description	Knots	Mph	Km/h
0	Calm	<1	<1	<1
1	Light air	1-3	1-3	1-5
2	Light breeze	4-6	4-7	6-11
3	Gentle breeze	7-10	8-12	12-19
4	Moderate breeze	11-16	13-18	20-29
5	Fresh breeze	17-21	19-24	30-39
6	Strong breeze	22-27	25-31	40-50
7	Moderate gale (Near gale)	28-33	32-38	51-61
8	Fresh gale	34-40	39-46	62-74
9	Strong gale	41-47	47-54	75-88
10	Whole gale	48-55	55-63	89-102
11	Storm	56-63	64-72	103-116
12	Hurricane	>63	>72	>117

Discussion
Also see questions embedded in Procedure.
1. Why does it matter where we take our wind readings? [Wind varies with height and closeness to buildings or other large objects.]
2. What effect does the force of the wind have on the ribbon? [The stronger the wind, the more the ribbon flies straight out or parallel to the ground.]
3. What other kinds of objects are used to show how the wind is blowing? [wind socks, weather vanes, etc.]
4. I wonder how we can take measurements of the wind. What are your ideas?

 Journal prompt: Describe a walk on a windy day. How did it feel? What did you see?

Extensions
1. Compare your wind direction data with data reported on weather radio, television, or websites for the same time. For example, if the National Weather Service reports wind coming from the northeast, did your wind detector give you the same results? If the results are different, why might they be different? (Examples: The weather station is many kilometers or miles from our school so the wind may blow differently there. We don't have a big, open space in which to take wind readings so nearby buildings might affect our results.)

2. Using data reported by the media and data gathered with your ribbon wind detector, attach a range of miles per hour for each number on your wind force scale. (There could be cause for some debate.) For example, if you recorded a light breeze (2 on your scale) and the National Weather Service stated wind speed at that same time was 8 miles per hour, you might determine that a light wind on your scale was roughly equivalent to 4-12 miles per hour or some other range of numbers. It would take many checks of data to establish the lower and upper ends of these ranges.

3. On a map of the school grounds, have students draw arrows to show wind direction (where it is coming from) at different locations. Data should be gathered at the same time from agreed-upon locations. Students can see wind flow around buildings as well as out in the open.

Curriculum Correlation
Literature
   Read one of the several books about wind listed in *Weather Literature* at the back of this book.

* Reprinted with permission from *Principles and Standards for School Mathematics,* 2000 by the National Council of Teachers of Mathematics. All rights reserved.

Connections
   The Earth heats unequally, due to its tilt as it revolves around the sun. This causes differences in air pressure and air pressure variations cause the air to move—wind. The greater the air pressure differences, the stronger the wind. By using the ribbon anemometer, students have informally observed that wind direction and wind speed vary. They have also been introduced to the historic *Beaufort Scale* and seen pictorial evidence that wind can cause damage.

   But a qualitative form of measuring is subjective and inexact. In the next two activities, we will move to a quantitative and more precise means of measuring wind direction (*Wind Ways)* and wind speed (*Just a Gust?).*

It's a Breeze!

Observe your wind detector at different heights.

... on the ground ... at shoulder height ... on a meter stick high above you

Observe it in different places.

... between buildings ... on different sides of a building ... under a tree ... in the open

Observe it at several different times.

What does your wind detector tell you about the wind?

Make a wind force scale by sketching how the ribbon looks in different amounts of wind.

Wind Force Scale

0	1	2	3

It's a Breeze!

Date/Time	Wind Direction	Wind Force Scale

```
           N
    NW          NE

    W     •     E

    SW          SE
           S
The wind is coming from the _____ .
```

```
           N
    NW          NE

    W     •     E

    SW          SE
           S
The wind is coming from the _____ .
```

```
           N
    NW          NE

    W     •     E

    SW          SE
           S
The wind is coming from the _____ .
```

```
           N
    NW          NE

    W     •     E

    SW          SE
           S
The wind is coming from the _____ .
```

```
           N
    NW          NE

    W     •     E

    SW          SE
           S
The wind is coming from the _____ .
```

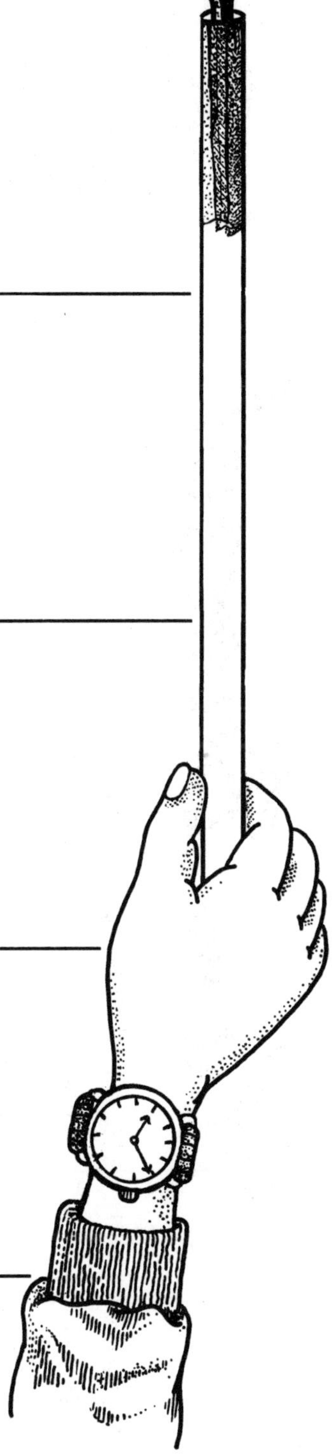

Beaufort Scale

In 1806 Sir Francis Beaufort (1774-1857), an Irish admiral in the British navy, developed a way to classify wind force at sea. For each number on the Beaufort (bō' fərt) Scale, he described the effect of the wind on the sails of a large ship (man-of-war). Descriptions of the effect of wind on land were eventually added. Over 100 years later wind speeds, measured in knots or nautical miles per hour, were added to the scale. Knots have been converted to miles per hour (mph) here since this is the common measure used in the United States.

Today official wind data are gathered by scientific measuring instruments rather than by observation of the winds' effects. However, the scale is fun to use for informal comparisons.

These numbers represent the miles per hour (mph) for each category of the Beaufort Scale. Cut and glue them in the proper order on the scale.

25-31	4-7
55-63	32-38
<1	13-18
19-24	39-46
1-3	8-12
>72	64-72

These pictures illustrate the effects of wind on land for each category of the Beaufort Scale. Cut and glue them in proper order on the scale.

Beaufort Scale

Number	Description	Mph	Effects on Land	Picture
0	Calm		Smoke rises straight up	
1	Light air		Smoke drifts; tree leaves barely move; wind vane doesn't move	
2	Light breeze		Leaves rustle; wind felt on face; wind vane moves	
3	Gentle breeze		Leaves and twigs move; bits of paper and dust rise from the ground	
4	Moderate breeze		Small branches move; raises dust and loose paper	
5	Fresh breeze		Small trees sway	
6	Strong breeze		Large branches sway; difficult to use umbrellas	
7	Moderate gale (Near gale)		Whole trees in motion; difficult to walk	
8	Fresh gale		Twigs break off trees	
9	Strong gale	47-54	Branches break; slight damage to buildings	
10	Whole gale		Trees blown down; heavy damage to buildings	
11	Storm		Widespread damage	
12	Hurricane		Extreme damage	

Topic
Weather station: wind direction

Key Question
What are the wind direction patterns in our area?

Focus
Students will build a wind vane and take wind direction readings over several weeks. The data will be graphed on a wind rose and used to determine dominant wind direction(s) for their location.

Guiding Documents
Project 2061 Benchmarks
* *Air is a substance that surrounds us, takes up space, and whose movement we feel as wind.*
* *Things change in steady, repetitive, or irregular ways—or sometimes in more than one way at the same time. Often the best way to tell which kinds of change are happening is to make a table or graph of measurements.*

NRC Standards
* *Employ simple equipment and tools to gather data and extend the senses.*
* *Weather changes from day to day and over the seasons. Weather can be described by measurable quantities, such as temperature, wind direction and speed, and precipitation.*

NCTM Standards 2000*
* *Describe location and movement using common language and geometric vocabulary*
* *Collect data using observations, surveys, and experiments*
* *Represent data using tables and graphs such as line plots, bar graphs, and line graphs*

Math
Geometry and measurement
    direction (angle)
Graphing
    bar: wind rose

Science
Earth science
    meteorology

Integrated Processes
Observing
Collecting and recording data
Comparing and contrasting
Interpreting data

Materials
Wooden or plastic ruler with a hole in the middle
Posterboard or non-corrugated cardboard
Dowel, 1 inch thick, about 12 inches long
1 nail at least 2 inches long
1 wooden bead, $\frac{3}{4}$ to 1 inch thick
2 small washers
Scissors
Hammer
Magnetic compass
Paper clips or clay
Masking tape
Crayons or colored pencils

Background Information
Wind is moving air. We have wind because of differences in the heating of the Earth which, in turn, causes differences in air pressure. Air moves from areas of high pressure toward areas of low pressure in an attempt to reach equilibrium.

Meteorologists measure the direction from which the wind is coming, not where it is going. Wind direction is identified using wind vanes and reported as one of the eight directions of a compass (N, NE, E, SE, S, SW, W, NW).

The tail of a wind vane needs to have a larger surface area than the arrow. The arrow will then point directly into the wind, registering from which direction the wind is coming. Be aware that wind vanes can be prone to error, as they may overshoot or swing past the true wind direction.

Meteorologists, if possible, mount wind measuring instruments on towers about 10 meters (33 feet) above the ground. The towers minimize the effects of obstacles, such as trees and buildings, or terrain on the wind. The height specifications were established by the World Meteorological Organization in 1971.

A special kind of bar graph, called a wind rose, visually relates wind direction data to the eight key points of a compass. Over time, dominant wind patterns for a location begin to emerge. These wind patterns are determined by global wind patterns as well as the geography of the land. Sudden shifts in wind may be significant predictors of changing weather.

Management

1. You are strongly encouraged to do the preliminary activity (see *Procedure*). Allow sufficient time for design and modifications. If the wind is calm during testing, a blow dryer or fan located a meter or more away can be used to simulate the wind.

2. The wind vane can be constructed beforehand. The arrow and tail should be laminated to protect from wet weather. Once attached, tape may be added to secure their position on the ruler. To balance the wind vane, tape paper clips or clay to the arrow side of the ruler. The wind vane can then be taped to the upper part of a fence.

3. In this activity, the wind vane is constructed from wood. A less durable wind vane made with a pencil, pushpin, straw, and tagboard may suffice in areas with low amounts of wind.

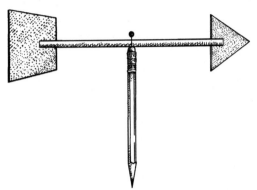

4. It is simplest to orientate the compass rose by using magnetic north (where the compass points), realizing that the direction will be somewhat of an approximation. Most locations in the continental United States will not vary more than 20° from geographical north. If you know the declination for your area, found on topographical maps, you can adjust the magnetic compass to geographical north. Another way to determine geographical north is by the layout of the streets. Streets in flat areas tend to be built along north/south and east/west lines.

5. Wind direction data should be taken once or maybe twice daily. During periods of unusual weather, more frequent readings may be desirable.

6. For added interest, make a classroom wind rose corresponding to the individual student graphs. Attach the *Wind Rose Base* to the center of a bulletin board or other display area. As data are collected, date a small sticky note and place it along the appropriate direction arm. Align the sticky notes along their short edges for consistent increments.

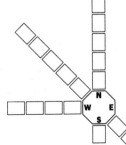

Procedure

Open-ended preliminary activity

1. Invite students to design, construct, and test their own wind vanes to find which works best. There are two options: 1) Have students design the entire wind vane, deciding what materials to use, how to make an arm that swings freely, whether to use an arrow or a tail or both, and the size and shape of the arrow and tail. 2) Have students use the straw wind vane (see *Management 3*) and experiment only with the arrow and tail, whether both are needed and their size and shape.

2. Discuss the design process and what was discovered.

Wind Vane

1. Ask, "From what direction do you think the wind blows at our school? Do you think it always blows from the same direction?"

2. Explain that today the class is going to keep track of wind direction for _____ (several weeks, the rest of the year, etc.) A wind vane will be added to the weather station.

3. Take the class to the location where the wind vane will be mounted. Tell them that buildings and other large objects can change the flow of the wind (as they observed in *It's a Breeze*) so it needs to be measured in an open place. Meteorologists also measure it well above the ground.

4. Attach the wind vane to the top of the fence and observe its direction. Have students use the magnetic compass to determine north and then the direction the wind vane is pointing. Explain that this is the direction from which the wind is coming, which is what meteorologists report. (In contrast, the ribbon wind detector in *It's a Breeze* shows which way the wind is going so students must determine from where it is coming.)

5. Lead the class back to the room, distribute the recording page, and have them write the date, time, wind direction, and weather (clear, partly cloudy, clouds increasing, storm coming, etc.)

6. Show students how wind direction is illustrated on the station model, using just the bar. For more information, see the *Station Model* activity.

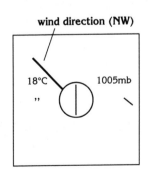

wind direction (NW)

7. Once all the intended data are gathered, say for the month, introduce students to the wind rose. Instruct students to count the number for each direction and color the graph.

8. After several weeks, discuss the wind patterns that are emerging. Statements can be recorded on chart paper. You might want to make a wind rose for each month and compare. The wind rose can be cut out so only the colored arms remain, making the pattern more visible. It can then be mounted on construction paper.

Discussion

Open-ended preliminary activity

1. What problems did you have to solve to make a working wind vane? [using the right materials, how to make an arm that moves freely, what the wind needs to blow against to make the arm move, the size and shape of the arrow and tail, etc.]

2. How did you solve each of these problems?
   a. What materials worked? [What materials work depend on the strength of the winds in your area. Fragile materials will be destroyed in strong winds. Heavy materials will not move easily.]
   b. How did you make an arm that moves freely? [A successful design will have as little friction as possible.]
   c. What was needed for the wind to make the arm move? Could you use just an arrow? [Both an arrow and a tail are needed.]
   d. What did you learn about the size and shape of the arrow and tail? [The tail should have a larger area than the arrow, in order for it to point to the direction from which the wind is coming.]

3. What things did you try that did not work well? (Learning often takes place by finding what did not work, then making modifications and testing again. Encourage their discussion of this process as a valued part of the experience.)

Wind Vane

1. What does a wind vane show? [from what direction the wind is coming (not where it is going)]

2. What are the wind patterns in our area for this month? Do the winds come mostly from one direction? What do you predict the wind patterns will be for next month?

3. How do our readings compare to those of the nearest National Weather Service station (or another published source)?

4. Is the kind of weather related to the direction of the wind? (consult data) If we know the wind direction, can we predict the weather? (relate back to *Wind Proverbs*)

Extensions

1. Once students know how to read wind data on a station model, they can use surface maps (see *Weather Websites*) to compare wind directions across part or all of the United States.

2. Compare data to the proverbs about wind directions.

3. Challenge: Look at a map of high and low pressure areas. How is wind direction in your area related to the nearest high and low? (Is the wind moving from low to high pressure or from high to low pressure?) [Movement is generally from high pressure to low pressure.]

* Reprinted with permission from *Principles and Standards for School Mathematics,* 2000 by the National Council of Teachers of Mathematics. All rights reserved.

Connections

The unequal heating of the Earth causes air pressure differences which, in turn, cause wind. A wind vane and a magnetic compass are used to note from which direction the wind is coming. Wind speed is a tandem measurement, addressed in the next activity, *Just a Gust?*

Wind Ways

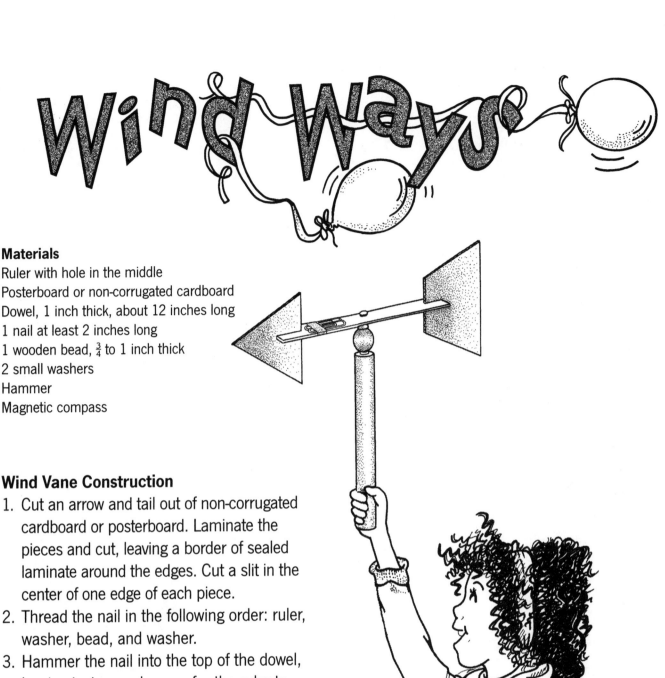

Materials
Ruler with hole in the middle
Posterboard or non-corrugated cardboard
Dowel, 1 inch thick, about 12 inches long
1 nail at least 2 inches long
1 wooden bead, $\frac{3}{4}$ to 1 inch thick
2 small washers
Hammer
Magnetic compass

Wind Vane Construction
1. Cut an arrow and tail out of non-corrugated cardboard or posterboard. Laminate the pieces and cut, leaving a border of sealed laminate around the edges. Cut a slit in the center of one edge of each piece.
2. Thread the nail in the following order: ruler, washer, bead, and washer.
3. Hammer the nail into the top of the dowel, leaving just enough room for the ruler to move freely.
4. Slide the arrow and tail, one onto each end of the ruler. Balance with clay or paper clips.

Wind Vane Location
Place the wind vane in an open area, away from buildings or other obstructions, and at least 1.5 meters above the ground.

Wind Ways

What are the wind direction patterns in our area?

Record the wind direction and graph on the wind rose.

Day	Time	Wind Direction	Weather

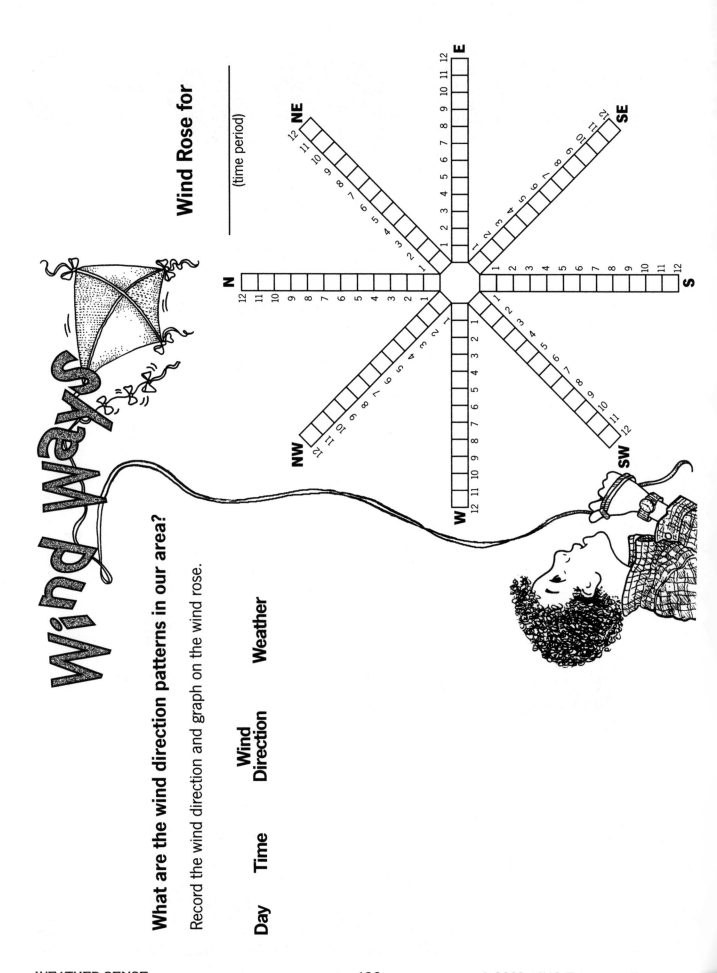

Wind Rose for

_____
(time period)

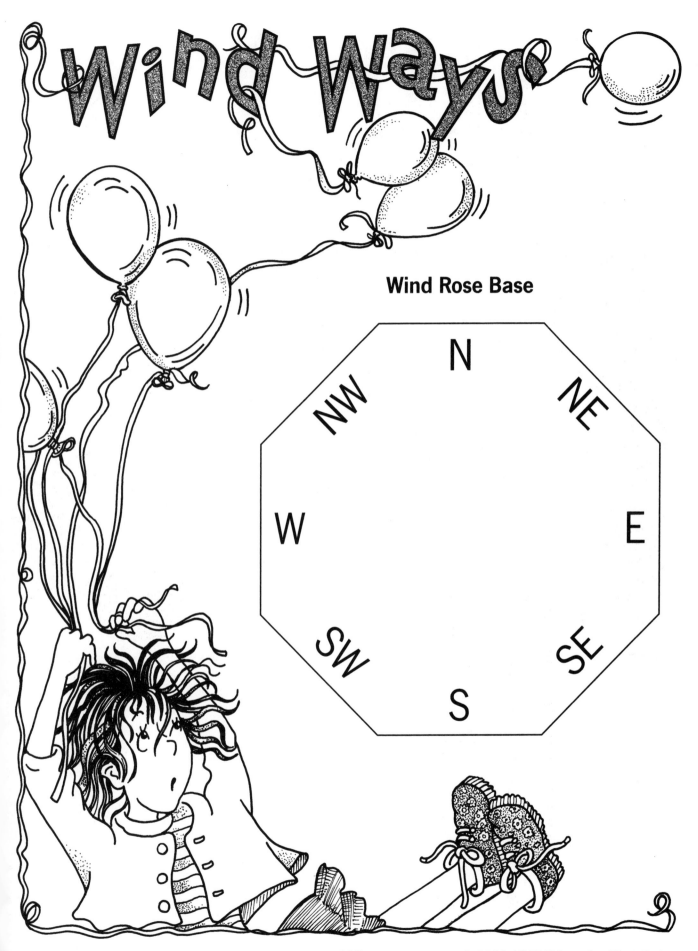

Wind Rose Base

N

NW

NE

W

E

SW

SE

S

JUST A GUST?

Topic
Weather station: wind speed

Key Question
How strong are the winds in our area?

Focus
Students will build an anemometer to detect wind speed and graph data to determine wind speed patterns at their location.

Guiding Documents
Project 2061 Benchmarks
- *Air is a substance that surrounds us, takes up space, and whose movement we feel as wind.*
- *Things change in steady, repetitive, or irregular ways—or sometimes in more than one way at the same time. Often the best way to tell which kinds of change are happening is to make a table or graph of measurements.*
- *Use numerical data in describing and comparing objects and events.*

NRC Standards
- *Employ simple equipment and tools to gather data and extend the senses.*
- *Weather changes from day to day and over the seasons. Weather can be described by measurable quantities, such as temperature, wind direction and speed, and precipitation.*

NCTM Standards 2000*
- *Select and apply appropriate standard units and tools to measure length, area, volume, weight, time, temperature, and the size of angles*
- *Collect data using observations, surveys, and experiments*
- *Represent data using tables and graphs such as line plots, bar graphs, and line graphs*

Math
Measurement
    angle
    estimation
Graphing
    bar to broken-line

Science
Earth science
    meteorology

Integrated Processes
Observing
Collecting and recording data
Comparing and contrasting
Interpreting data
Relating

Materials
Cardstock for protractor
60 cm of thread
Tape or glue
Table tennis ball
Straight stick
Bubble level (see *Management 2*)

Background Information
Because of the tilt of the Earth as it revolves around the sun and because land and water absorb heat energy at different rates, the Earth's surface is heated unequally. Cool air has higher pressure while warm air has lower pressure. Differences in the pressure of neighboring air masses set the air in motion. High-pressure air moves toward low-pressure air, trying to equalize the air pressure.

How fast the wind blows depends on the distance between high- and low-pressure air masses and the amount of difference in air pressure. On a surface weather map, this is illustrated by the locations of the high- and low-pressure systems and the spacing between the isobars. The closer the two pressure systems and the greater the temperature/air pressure difference (the closer the isobars), the stronger the force of the wind.

A three- or four-cup anemometer is commonly used by meteorologists to gather official wind data. It is positioned in an open area and at a height of 10 meters (about 33 feet). To accommodate the school setting, the protractor anemometer constructed here should be placed off the ground at a reasonable height, say, above the shoulders. Point the protractor anemometer directly into the wind.

Management
1. Choose the protractor that best suits your students' needs and make copies on cardstock. The mph-km/h protractor permits direct readings. The traditional protractor provides practice in reading angles and then consulting a table to determine wind speed.
2. Inexpensive rectangular tube levels are available at AIMS. They can also be found at hardware and home-building stores.
3. While only one anemometer is necessary for the weather station, you may want to have several so all students can gain sufficient experience using it. If using one anemometer, assemble it beforehand. If using several, have students groups assemble the anemometers as part of the activity.
4. This activity builds on the observations made with the ribbon wind detector in *It's a Breeze!* Consider doing that activity first if you have not already done so.

Procedure

1. Ask the *Key Question*, "How strong are the winds in our area?" (Expect qualitative responses such as "The wind blows hard" or "We don't have much wind" more than quantitative responses quoting ___ miles-per-hour.) Explain that wind speed is one of the readings taken at a weather station. Students will be using an anemometer, an instrument which measures the strength or speed of wind, to gather data.

2. Introduce the anemometer you constructed or have student groups assemble their own using the construction page directions. Explain that in order to take valid measurements, the protractor (either one) must form an angle with one ray—the stick—parallel to the ground and the other ray—the thread—perpendicular to the ground when there is no wind. Demonstrate how to use the bubble level to properly position the stick.

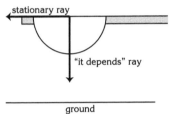

3. Take the class out into an open area and have them point the anemometer *into* the wind while keeping the bubble in the level at the center mark. Instruct students to read the wind speed directly (mph or km/h protractor) or read the angle and consult the wind speed table (degree protractor).

4. Distribute the recording page and have students make a table of data, several times during the day or once each day for a week or more. Include date, time, degrees (if used), and wind speed.

5. After students have made a bar graph, guide them through the directions for representing the same data as a broken-line graph.

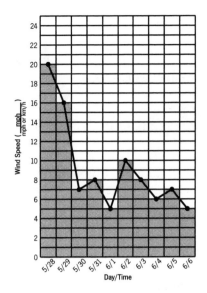

6. Discuss the wind patterns. Decide how often wind speed readings will be taken for the weather station—once a day, twice a day, or hourly.

7. Add wind speed data to the wind bar on the station model. (See *Station Model*.)

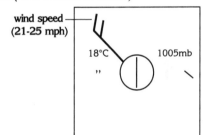

Discussion

1. What kind of wind speed patterns do we have, if any? Does the wind get stronger at certain times of the day? Is it more windy at certain times of the year?

2. Examine other data you have gathered from your weather station. When there is a change in wind speed, is there also a change in any other readings? (Relate to air pressure and temperature.)

 Journal prompt: Make a list of words that describe or are synonyms of wind. Use some of these words to write a poem about wind.

Extension

Compare wind speeds around the country by reading surface maps at weather websites.

Connections

Air pressure variations, due to the unequal heating of the Earth, cause the air to move. The greater the pressure differences and/or the shorter the distance between a high pressure system and a neighboring low pressure system, the stronger the winds. Students can use a protractor anemometer to quantitatively measure wind strength.

Wind causes the temperature to feel cooler. This effect, of particular interest during the winter when frostbite and hypothermia can be safety concerns, is explored in *Chillin' in the Wind*.

JUST A GUST?

Protractors

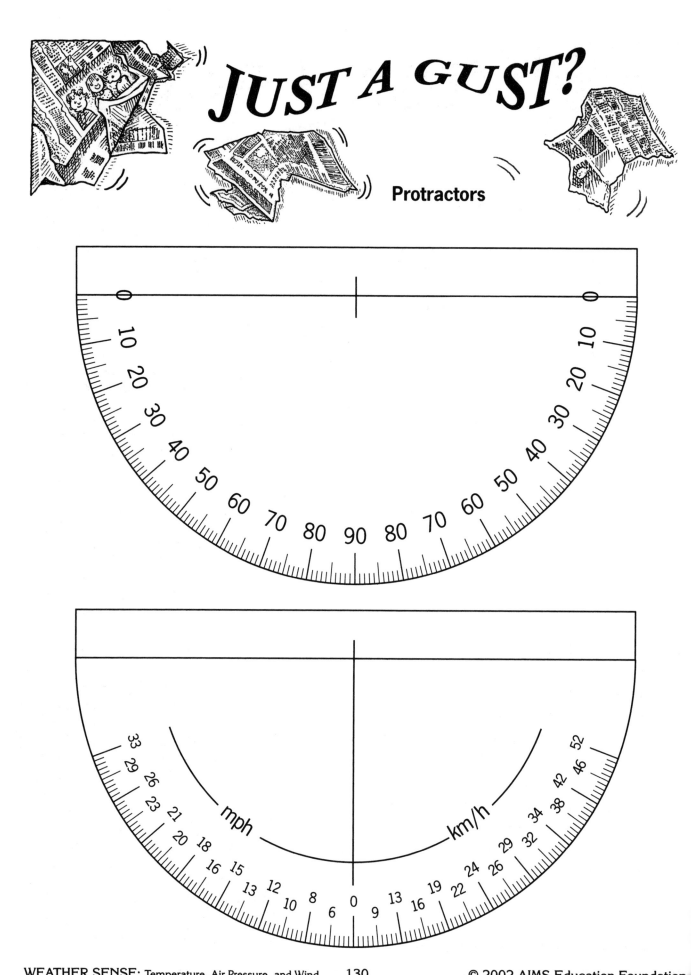

JUST A GUST?

Building an anemometer

Materials
60 cm of thread
Tape or glue
Table tennis ball
Straight stick
Bubble level

| | Wind Speed* | |
Angle	Mph	Km/h
90°	0	0
85°	6	9
80°	8	13
75°	10	16
70°	12	19
65°	13	22
60°	15	24
55°	16	26
50°	18	29
45°	20	32
40°	21	34
35°	23	38
30°	26	42
25°	29	46
20°	33	52

1. Cut out the protractor. Poke a very small hole where the lines intersect at the top center of the protractor. Push the thread through the hole and glue or tape to the back.
2. Glue or tape the protractor to a straight stick. Tape the other end of the thread to the ball.
3. Glue or tape the bubble level to the top of the stick. When level, the thread should hang straight down the center line, 90° or 0 depending on the protractor used.
4. Out in an open area, point the stick into the wind while keeping the bubble in the level at the center mark.
5. For the miles-per-hour or kilometers-per-hour protractor, record day/time and wind speed. For the angle protractor, record day/time, angle, and wind speed using the table to the right.

*Suzuki, David. *Looking at Weather.* John Wiley & Sons, Inc. New York. 1991.

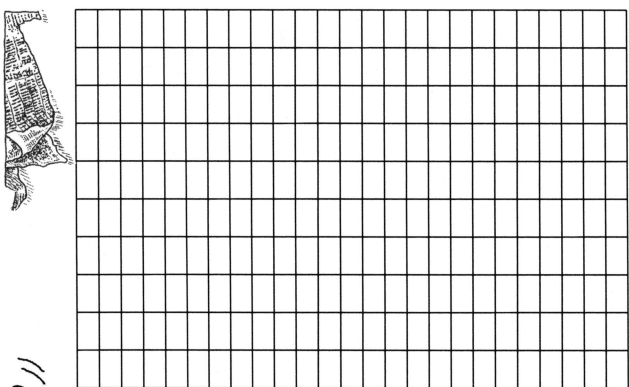

Day/Time

JUST A GUST?

Wind Speed (——————)
mph or km/h

Record wind speed data.

Make a bar graph.
Put a dot at the top center of each colored bar.
Connect the dots to make a broken-line graph.

What does the graph tell you?

Chillin' in the Wind

Topic
Wind chill

Key Question
How does wind affect how cold it feels?

Focus
Students will gather temperature and wind speed data, then use a wind chill table to determine how cold the air feels. Clothing choices, types of exercise, and other safety precautions will be discussed.

Guiding Documents
Project 2061 Benchmarks
- Air is a substance that surrounds us, takes up space, and whose movement we feel as wind.
- Use numerical data in describing and comparing objects and events.

NRC Standards
- Weather changes from day to day and over the seasons. Weather can be described by measurable quantities, such as temperature, wind direction and speed, and precipitation.
- Safety and security are basic needs of humans. Safety involves freedom from danger, risk, or injury. Security involves feelings of confidence and lack of anxiety and fear. Student understandings include following safety rules for home and school, preventing abuse and neglect, avoiding injury, knowing whom to ask for help, and when and how to say no.

NCTM Standards 2000*
- Select and apply appropriate standard units and tools to measure length, area, volume, weight, time, temperature, and the size of angles
- Collect data using observations, surveys, and experiments

Math
Measurement
    temperature
    angle (protractor anemometer)
Statistics

Science
Earth science
    meteorology

Integrated Processes
Observing
Collecting and recording data
Comparing and contrasting
Interpreting data
Relating

Materials
Thermometer
Protractor anemometer (see *Just a Gust?*)
Colored pencils

Background Information
Wind Chill

The human body has built-in temperature regulators. When we are warm, sweating cools us. When we are cold, shivering warms us. Blood vessels near the surface of the skin also constrict so the blood loses less heat to the air.

The human body is constantly radiating heat. If the air is still, the air warmed by the body stays next to it. But wind carries the warm air away from the body and makes a person feel colder than the thermometer shows. During cold weather, this is called wind chill. During warm weather, this effect is not referred to as "wind chill," even though it makes us feel cooler. Wind chill applies only to people and animals; non-living objects cannot be cooled lower than the actual temperature of the air.

The old wind chill formula, in use since it was developed in the 1940s, was based on experiments two scientists conducted in Antarctica in which they measured how long it took a can of water to freeze at various wind speeds and temperatures. Its validity, for a variety of reasons, has been questioned by atmospheric scientists for some time. In an effort to improve upon this formula, the National Weather Service (NWS) and the Meteorological Services of Canada (MSC) jointly developed a new wind chill formula, based on modern heat transfer theory, which went into use in fall 2001. The formula was verified through clinical testing, resulting in new wind chill tables which have been incorporated into this activity.

Effects of Extreme Wind Chill

Wind chill tables alert us to the need for bundling up, increasing exercise to compensate for heat loss, or reducing the time spent outdoors. Extra precautions should be taken with children, the elderly, and those who are ill. Unsafe conditions begin at about -25°C or about -18°F.

The two dangers of cold, windy temperatures are hypothermia and frostbite. If a person loses enough heat so that body temperature drops below about 95°F, hypothermia sets in. A person becomes confused and disoriented and may shiver violently at first. Unconsciousness and possibly death can follow. Prevention includes wearing layers of clothes. Outer garments should be tightly-woven, water-repellant, and hooded.

The combination of wind and cold air can remove heat so fast from the skin that it begins to freeze and discolor. Frostbite can lead to extreme sensitivity to cold or even the need for amputation. The most vulnerable parts of the body are the ears, nose, hands, and feet. Keep these body parts covered, warm, and dry. Hats, dry socks, and face coverings are helpful and, for hands, mittens are a better choice than gloves.

Management

1. Since wind chill applies only to cold temperatures, it is best to do this activity during the winter.
2. It is presumed that students are already acquainted with gathering temperature and wind speed data. (See *Temperature Tally* and *Just a Gust?* for more on these topics.)
3. Tables in both customary (Fahrenheit, miles-per-hour) and metric (Celsius, kilometers-per-hour) are provided. The tables are not conversions of each other but are based on increments appropriate to each measuring system. Use the table that corresponds with the measuring system you will use.

Procedure

1. Ask, "When you are outdoors, have you ever felt colder than what the temperature on the thermometer says?" Explain that there is a reason for that. The wind takes heat away from our bodies and we feel cooler than the actual temperature. In cold weather, this is called wind chill. We need to be aware of wind chill so we can protect ourselves when conditions become dangerous.

2. Distribute the chosen wind chill table and study it together. Suggest students color the unsafe temperatures in the table, as explained on the page. As an option, add a stair-step path separating the safe from the unsafe temperatures.

Air Temperature (°C)

Wind Speed (km/h)	5	0	-5	-10	-15	-20	-25	-30	-35	-40	-45	-50
5	4	-2	-7	-13	-19	-24	-30	-36	-41	-47	-53	-58
10	3	-3	-9	-15	-21	-27	-33	-39	-45	-51	-57	-63
15	2	-4	-11	-17	-23	-29	-35	-41	-48	-54	-60	-66
20	1	-5	-12	-18	-24	-31	-37	-43	-49	-56	-62	-68
25	1	-6	-12	-19	-25	-32	-38	-45	-51	-57	-64	-70
30	0	-7	-13	-20	-26	-33	-39	-46	-52	-59	-65	-72
35	0	-7	-14	-20	-27	-33	-40	-47	-53	-60	-66	-73
40	-1	-7	-14	-21	-27	-34	-41	-48	-54	-61	-68	-74
45	-1	-8	-15	-21	-28	-35	-42	-48	-55	-62	-69	-75
50	-1	-8	-15	-22	-29	-35	-42	-49	-56	-63	-70	-76

3. Have students gather air temperature and wind speed data, then determine the amount of wind chill using the table.
4. Discuss the effects dangerous wind chill can have on people (frostbite and hypothermia) and the safety precautions that can be taken. Precautions include the amount and kinds of clothing, kinds of exercise, and amount of time spent outdoors. Encourage students to talk about safety suggestions they have heard from other sources—parents, television weather reports, etc.

Discussion

Getting acquainted with the wind chill table

1. What weather conditions will give a "0" wind chill temperature?
   [Metric: 5°C and 30 km/h; 5° and 35 km/h]
   [Customary: 20°F and 35 mph; 15°F and 15 mph]
2. Metric: If the air temperature is -10°C and the wind speed is 50 km/h, what is the wind chill? [-22°C]
   Customary: If the air temperature is 15°F and the wind speed is 45 mph, what is the wind chill? [-9°F]
3. Metric: Which combination produces a colder wind chill temperature, a 10 km/h wind at -15°C or a 25 km/h wind at -10°C? [10 km/h wind at -15°C (wind chill of -21°C) as opposed to a wind chill of -19°C for the other combination]
   Customary: Which combination produces a colder wind chill temperature, a 40 mph wind at 25°F or a 30 mph wind at 15°F? [30 mph wind at 15°F (wind chill of -5°F) as opposed to a wind chill of 6°F for the other combination]

General questions

1. Did the wind affect how cold the temperature feels today? Explain. [Examples: No, there wasn't enough wind to make a difference. Yes, the wind was blowing quite hard, about 20 kilometers per hour.] What temperature difference did it make? (Compare air temperature to wind chill temperature.)

2. How safe is the wind chill today? How can you protect yourself when the wind chill becomes dangerous? [wear layers of clothing; cover the face, hands, head, and feet; if going outside, keep moving—actively exercise; limit time spent outdoors]

Extension

If your weather is not cool or windy enough, adopt another city and gather temperature and wind speed data from a weather website.

Curriculum Correlation

Art

Have students make posters illustrating safety precautions during dangerous wind chill temperatures.

* Reprinted with permission from *Principles and Standards for School Mathematics,* 2000 by the National Council of Teachers of Mathematics. All rights reserved.

Connections

Wind speed has a cooling effect on how the temperature feels to us. The stronger the wind, the more it chills. The link between wind speed and the perceived temperature illustrates the interaction between the four elements of weather—temperature, air pressure, wind, and moisture. No one element operates in isolation.

We have examined the effects of wind through the past several activities. The next page after this activity offers suggestions for assessing what has been learned.

© 2002 AIMS Education Foundation

Chillin' in the Wind

Wind Chill Equivalent Temperature

Wind chill is not an actual temperature reading but a way of expressing how cold the wind makes us feel. Wind evaporates moisture more quickly and removes the heated layer of air near the body.

Air Temperature (°C)

Wind Speed (km/h)	5	0	-5	-10	-15	-20	-25	-30	-35	-40	-45	-50
5	4	-2	-7	-13	-19	-24	-30	-36	-41	-47	-53	-58
10	3	-3	-9	-15	-21	-27	-33	-39	-45	-51	-57	-63
15	2	-4	-11	-17	-23	-29	-35	-41	-48	-54	-60	-66
20	1	-5	-12	-18	-24	-31	-37	-43	-49	-56	-62	-68
25	1	-6	-12	-19	-25	-32	-38	-45	-51	-57	-64	-70
30	0	-7	-13	-20	-26	-33	-39	-46	-52	-59	-65	-72
35	0	-7	-14	-20	-27	-33	-40	-47	-53	-60	-66	-73
40	-1	-7	-14	-21	-27	-34	-41	-48	-54	-61	-68	-74
45	-1	-8	-15	-21	-28	-35	-42	-48	-55	-62	-69	-75
50	-1	-8	-15	-22	-29	-35	-42	-49	-56	-63	-70	-76

At about -25°C, there is risk of frostbite with prolonged exposure. Color the wind chill temperatures at or below -25°C.

How can you protect yourself from cold, windy weather?

Chillin' in the Wind

Wind Chill Equivalent Temperature

Wind chill is not an actual temperature reading but a way of expressing how cold the wind makes us feel. Wind evaporates moisture more quickly and removes the heated layer of air near the body.

Air Temperature (°F)

Wind Speed (mph)	30	25	20	15	10	5	0	-5	-10	-15	-20	-25	30
5	25	19	13	7	1	-5	-11	-16	-22	-28	-34	-40	-46
10	21	15	9	3	-4	-10	-16	-22	-28	-35	-41	-47	-53
15	19	13	6	0	-7	-13	-19	-26	-32	-39	-45	-51	-58
20	17	11	4	-2	-9	-15	-22	-29	-35	-42	-48	-55	-61
25	16	9	3	-4	-11	-17	-24	-31	-37	-44	-51	-58	-64
30	15	8	1	-5	-12	-19	-26	-33	-39	-46	-53	-60	-67
35	14	7	0	-7	-14	-21	-27	-34	-41	-48	-55	-62	-69
40	13	6	-1	-8	-15	-22	-29	-36	-43	-50	-57	-64	-71
45	12	5	-2	-9	-16	-23	-30	-37	-44	-51	-58	-65	-72
50	12	4	-3	-10	-17	-24	-31	-38	-45	-52	-60	-67	-74

At about -18°F, there is risk of frostbite with prolonged exposure. Color the wind chill temperatures at or below -18°F.

How can you protect yourself from cold, windy weather?

Wind Assessment

Essential Question

What are the effects of wind?

Learning Goals

- Observe and gather evidence, both qualitative and quantitative, that wind varies in direction and speed.
- Understand that, under certain conditions, wind can cause safety concerns for people and/or property.

Wind Assessment

Activity

This is an informal assessment of group and class learning, rather than individual learning. Since the effects of wind are observational, pictures and words serve this assessment. Have students draw a windy scene or write a poem about the effects of wind. Assemble students in groups of five or six and have them physically order their pictures and/or poems from mild winds to strong winds. When the groups have completed their tasks, encourage them to walk around the room and examine other groups' results in a peer-to-peer assessment.

As a class, take all of the creative work and ask students to order it on the wall from gentle to gale force.

Discussion

1. How difficult was it to decide the order of the pictures/poems in your group? Explain.
   [• Easy. Every picture showed a different wind speed.
   • A little hard. In two pictures, the wind strength looked about the same so we had to decide which would be first and which would be second.
   • We had problems. A poem mentioned both mild and strong winds so we weren't sure where to place it. Several pictures showed about the same strength of wind so we didn't know which to put first.]
2. Did you agree with the picture/poem order chosen by other groups? Explain.
3. How can our class picture/poem order be related to the Beaufort Scale?

Evidence of Learning

Peer-to-peer evaluation of group picture sequences requires students to use their own learning to judge the results. Teacher assessment involves circulating among groups and listening or asking questions about the order that was chosen. Look for illustrations of the wind's effects:
- the motion of leaves, a kite, towels on a clothesline, etc.
- damage to trees, buildings, etc.
- the temperature feeling colder because of wind

Weather Literature

General   Fisher, Aileen. *Always Wondering*. HarperCollins. New York. 1991. (The last section of this book, "Whoever Planned the World," has several wonderful poems having to do with weather.)

Kahl, Jonathan D. W. *National Audubon Society First Field Guide: Weather*. Scholastic, Inc. New York. 1998. (An introduction to weather, loaded with photographs and information. Includes a pictorial field guide card for handy identification of phenomena.)

Yolen, Jane, ed. *Weather Report: Poems Selected by Jane Yolen*. Boyds Mills Press (A Highlights Co.). Honesdale, PA. 1993. (Inviting poetry organized around the topics of rain, sun, wind, snow, and fog.)

Temperature   Silverstein, Shel. "Here Comes," "Come Skating," "Tryin' on Clothes," and "It's Hot!" from *A Light in the Attic*. Harper & Row. New York. 1981. (Poetry with a unique twist of humor.)

Wind   Bauer, Caroline Feller, ed. *Windy Day: Stories and Poems*. J.B. Lippincott. New York. 1988. (Delightful titles such as "While You Were Chasing a Hat!" and "The Bagel" are found in this collection of stories and poems.)

Calhoun, Mary. *Jack and the Whoopee Wind*. William Morrow. New York. 1987. (A whimsical tall tale about Cowboy Jack's attempts to stop the wind from blowing everything away. Great fun.)

Carlstrom, Nancy White. *How Does the Wind Walk?* Macmillan. New York. 1993. (Simple but poetic words and colorful illustrations about a young boy encountering the effects of the wind in each of the seasons.)

Ets, Marie Hall. *Gilberto and the Wind*. Viking Press. New York. 1963. (A young boy experiences the playfulness of wind in different settings and at different times of the year.)

Kennedy, Dorothy M., ed. *Make Things Fly: Poems about the Wind*. Margaret K. McElderry Books (Simon & Schuster). New York. 1998. (This collection of poems includes two appealing activity-openers, "Crick! Crack!" by Eve Merriam and "The Wind" by John Ciardi.)

MacDonald, Elizabeth. *The Very Windy Day*. Tambourine Books (William Morrow). New York. 1991. (An amusing story in which the wind blows a hat and other objects away from people, passing the objects from person to person, and eventually returning them to their owners.)

McKissack, Patricia C. *Mirandy and Brother Wind*. Alfred A. Knopf. New York. 1988. (Mirandy tries to capture Brother Wind so that he can be her partner in the Junior Cakewalk Dance Contest.)

Silverstein, Shel. "Strange Wind" from *A Light in the Attic*. Harper & Row. New York. 1981. (Poetry with a unique twist of humor.)

Water Cycle

Branley, Franklin M. *Down Comes the Rain*. Scholastic, Inc. New York. 2000. (Drawn pictures explain evaporation, condensation, and precipitation. Though the look is primary, conceptually it is appropriate for middle grades, too.)

Markert, Jenny. *Water*. Creative Education, Inc. Mankato, MN. 1992. (Informative text and gorgeous full-page colored photographs of scenes illustrating the water cycle as well as weathering caused by water in both its solid and liquid forms.)

McKinney, Barbara Shaw. *A Drop Around the World*. Dawn Publications. Nevada City, CA. 1998. (Colorful drawings and narrative in the form of verse illustrate how a drop of water continually changes form—becoming part of a cloud, rain, the ocean, a snow-flake, the soil, the jet stream, the rain forest, etc. Excellent for middle grades, with a natural connection to geography.)

Waldman, Neil. *The Snowflake: A Water Cycle Story*. The Millbrook Press. Brookfield, Connecticut. 2003. (Follow the journey of a snowflake through the changing phases of the water cycle—frozen pond, underground stream, irrigation system, cloud, ocean, etc. Inviting two-page drawings are keyed to the months of the year and accompanied by a brief descriptive text.)

Walker, Sally M. *Water Up, Water Down: The Hydrologic Cycle*. Carolrhoda Books, Inc. Minneapolis. 1992. (Beautiful photographs accompany a text explaining the water cycle.)

Wick, Walter. *A Drop of Water*. Scholastic Press. Jefferson City, MO. 1996. (Text and wonderful photographs that illustrate the properties of water as well as the water cycle. Includes snowflakes, condensation, and evaporation. Suitable for middle grades and beyond.)

Clouds

Ariane. *Small Cloud*. Walker and Company. New York. 1996. (An endearing tale of the birth of a cloud, its travels, and how it eventually fed the Earth with rain, completing a journey through the water cycle.)

Harper, Suzanne. *Clouds: From Mare's Tails to Thunderheads*. Franklin Watts. New York. 1997. (Basic information about clouds with text and photographs given about equal space.)

Lustig, Michael and Esther. *Willy Whyner, Cloud Designer*. Four Winds Press (Macmillan). New York. 1994. (A fantasy about a third-grade boy who makes unusual kinds of clouds. Tongue-in-cheek humor.)

McMillan, Bruce. *The Weather Sky*. Farrar Straus Giroux. New York. 1991. (Various kinds of clouds are introduced, each featured on a page with a color photograph, paragraph of text, and an altitude graph showing its relative position in the sky. For upper elementary and above.)

Markert, Jenny. *Clouds*. Creative Education, Inc. Mankato, MN. 1992. (Brief but informative text and gorgeous full-page colored photographs of the three types of clouds and associated weather phenomena. An excellent introduction for elementary students.)

de Paola, Tomie. *The Cloud Book*. Holiday House. New York. 1985 (reissue). (Cloud descriptions and a few weather proverbs provide the text for the colorful illustrations.)

Silverstein, Shel. "Arrows" from *A Light in the Attic*. Harper & Row. New York. 1981. (Poetry with a unique twist of humor.)

Rain

Bauer, Caroline Feller, ed. *Rainy Day: Stories and Poems*. HarperCollins. New York. 1986. (A collection with titles such as "Rain-Walking," "Rain Sizes," and "Cloudy with a Chance of Meatballs.")

Buchanan, Ken & Debby. *It Rained on the Desert Today*. Northland Publishing. Flagstaff, AZ. 1994. (The anticipation and wonder of a desert rain seen through the eyes of children. Beautiful watercolor illustrations. A "Reading Rainbow" book.)

Cobb, Vicki. *This Place is Dry*. Walker and Co. New York. 1989. (Become immersed in the dry climate, plants, and animals of Arizona's Sonoran Desert.)

Cobb, Vicki. *This Place is Wet*. Walker and Co. New York. 1989. (Colored drawings and text help you experience life in the Brazilian Rain Forest—the humid, wet climate, the people, the plants, and the animals.)

Silverstein, Shel. "Snap!" from *A Light in the Attic*. Harper & Row. New York. 1981. (Poetry with a unique twist of humor.)

Silverstein, Shel. "Rain" and "Lazy Jane" from *Where the Sidewalk Ends*. Harper & Row. New York. 1974. (Humorous poetry.)

Spier, Peter. *Rain*. Zephyr. Somerville, MA. 1987. (Two children enjoy the rain in this wordless book.)

Snow

Bauer, Caroline Feller, ed. *Snowy Day: Stories and Poems*. HarperCollins. New York. 1986. (A collection of short stories, poems, and a recipe or two to capture the imagination.)

Bianchi, John and Edwards, Frank B. *Snow*. Bungalo Books. Newburgh, Ontario, Canada or Firefly Books Inc. Buffalo, NY. 1992. (Inviting illustrations and varied content, from snowshoes to igloos to animals, draw you into "learning for the fun of it," the book's subtitle.)

Martin, Jacqueline Briggs. *Snowflake Bentley*. Houghton Mifflin. Boston. 1998. (Winner of the 1998 Caldecott Medal, this book introduces children to Wilson Bentley whose hobby was photographing snowflakes, thousands of them, in the early 1900s. Illustrated by Mary Azarian.)

McSwigan, Marie. *Snow Treasure*. Scholastic, Inc. New York. 1997 (reissue). (A suspenseful, though probably fictional, story set in Norway during World War II. Using the snowy winter landscape and their sleds, Norwegian children slip thousands of dollars of gold bricks past the German invaders.)

Prelutsky, Jack. *It's Snowing! It's Snowing!* Greenwillow Books. New York. 1984. (Whimsical poetry about everyday happenings in cold weather. Includes titles such as "The Snowman's Lament," "Stuck in the Snow," and "My Mother Took Me Skating." Perfect for middle grades.)

Silverstein, Shel. "Snowman" from *Where the Sidewalk Ends*. Harper & Row. New York. 1974. (Humorous poetry.)

Look for *The Winter of the Blue Snow*, a very short story about spoken words freezing in mid-air, in a number of books about Paul Bunyan.

Reference Books for Teachers

Ludlum, David M. *The Audubon Society Field Guide to North American Weather*. Alfred A. Knopf. New York. 1991. (Concise explanations, photographs to aid identification of clouds and other weather phenomena, information on weather instruments and the station model, etc.)

Williams, Jack. *The Weather Book (USA Today®)*. Vintage Books (Random House, Inc.). New York. 1992. (Explanations and extensive graphics make the complexities of weather understandable. If you only get one reference, this is the one to have.)

Weather Websites

For National Weather Service station sites:

NOAA*	http://www.nws.noaa.gov/organization.php
NOAA*	http://www.wrh.noaa.gov/wrh/nwspage.php

For current weather conditions:

AccuWeather	http://www.accuweather.com/
BBC Weather Centre	http://www.bbc.co.uk/weather/
Intellicast	http://www.intellicast.com/
The Weather Channel	http://www.weather.com/
USA Today	http://www.usatoday.com/weather/
Weather Office—Canada	http://www.weatheroffice.ec.gc.ca/
WeatherNet	http://cirrus.sprl.umich.edu/wxnet/
Weather Underground	http://www.wunderground.com/

For snow data:

NOAA*	http://lwf.ncdc.noaa.gov/oa/climate/research/snow/recent.html

For monthly climate data:

World Climate	http://www.worldclimate.com

For weather calculators:

NOAA*	http://www.srh.noaa.gov/elp/wxcalc/wxcalc.shtml

*National Oceanic and Atmospheric Administration
Correct at time of publication.

The AIMS Program

AIMS is the acronym for "Activities Integrating Mathematics and Science." Such integration enriches learning and makes it meaningful and holistic. AIMS began as a project of Fresno Pacific University to integrate the study of mathematics and science in grades K-9, but has since expanded to include language arts, social studies, and other disciplines.

AIMS is a continuing program of the non-profit AIMS Education Foundation. It had its inception in a National Science Foundation funded program whose purpose was to explore the effectiveness of integrating mathematics and science. The project directors in cooperation with 80 elementary classroom teachers devoted two years to a thorough field-testing of the results and implications of integration.

The approach met with such positive results that the decision was made to launch a program to create instructional materials incorporating this concept. Despite the fact that thoughtful educators have long recommended an integrative approach, very little appropriate material was available in 1981 when the project began. A series of writing projects have ensued, and today the AIMS Education Foundation is committed to continue the creation of new integrated activities on a permanent basis.

The AIMS program is funded through the sale of books, products, and staff development workshops and through proceeds from the Foundation's endowment. All net income from program and products flows into a trust fund administered by the AIMS Education Foundation. Use of these funds is restricted to support of research, development, and publication of new materials. Writers donate all their rights to the Foundation to support its on-going program. No royalties are paid to the writers.

The rationale for integration lies in the fact that science, mathematics, language arts, social studies, etc., are integrally interwoven in the real world from which it follows that they should be similarly treated in the classroom where we are preparing students to live in that world. Teachers who use the AIMS program give enthusiastic endorsement to the effectiveness of this approach.

Science encompasses the art of questioning, investigating, hypothesizing, discovering, and communicating. Mathematics is the language that provides clarity, objectivity, and understanding. The language arts provide us powerful tools of communication. Many of the major contemporary societal issues stem from advancements in science and must be studied in the context of the social sciences. Therefore, it is timely that all of us take seriously a more holistic mode of educating our students. This goal motivates all who are associated with the AIMS Program. We invite you to join us in this effort.

Meaningful integration of knowledge is a major recommendation coming from the nation's professional science and mathematics associations. The American Association for the Advancement of Science in *Science for All Americans* strongly recommends the integration of mathematics, science, and technology. The National Council of Teachers of Mathematics places strong emphasis on applications of mathematics such as are found in science investigations. AIMS is fully aligned with these recommendations.

Extensive field testing of AIMS investigations confirms these beneficial results:

1. Mathematics becomes more meaningful, hence more useful, when it is applied to situations that interest students.
2. The extent to which science is studied and understood is increased, with a significant economy of time, when mathematics and science are integrated.
3. There is improved quality of learning and retention, supporting the thesis that learning which is meaningful and relevant is more effective.
4. Motivation and involvement are increased dramatically as students investigate real-world situations and participate actively in the process.

We invite you to become part of this classroom teacher movement by using an integrated approach to learning and sharing any suggestions you may have. The AIMS Program welcomes you!

AIMS Education Foundation Programs

Practical proven strategies to improve student achievement

When you host an AIMS workshop for elementary and middle school educators, you will know your teachers are receiving effective usable training they can apply in their classrooms immediately.

Designed for teachers—AIMS Workshops:
- Correlate to your state standards;
- Address key topic areas, including math content, science content, problem solving, and process skills;
- Teach you how to use AIMS' effective hands-on approach;
- Provide practice of activity-based teaching;
- Address classroom management issues, higher-order thinking skills, and materials;
- Give you AIMS resources; and
- Offer college (graduate-level) credits for many courses.

Aligned to district and administrator needs—AIMS workshops offer:
- Flexible scheduling and grade span options;
- Custom (one-, two-, or three-day) workshops to meet specific schedule, topic and grade-span needs;
- Pre-packaged one-day workshops on most major topics—only $3,900 for up to 30 participants (includes all materials and expenses);
- Prepackaged *week-long* workshops (four- or five-day formats) for in-depth math and science training—only $12,300 for up to 30 participants (includes all materials and expenses);
- Sustained staff development, by scheduling workshops throughout the school year and including follow-up and assessment;
- Eligibility for funding under the Eisenhower Act and No Child Left Behind; and

- Affordable professional development—save when you schedule consecutive-day workshops.

University Credit—Correspondence Courses

AIMS offers correspondence courses through a partnership with Fresno Pacific University.
- Convenient distance-learning courses—you study at your own pace and schedule. No computer or Internet access required!

The tuition for each three-semester unit graduate-level course is $264 plus a materials fee.

The AIMS Instructional Leadership Program

This is an AIMS staff-development program seeking to prepare facilitators for leadership roles in science/math education in their home districts or regions. Upon successful completion of the program, trained facilitators become members of the AIMS Instructional Leadership Network, qualified to conduct AIMS workshops, teach AIMS in-service courses for college credit, and serve as AIMS consultants. Intensive training is provided in mathematics, science, process and thinking skills, workshop management, and other relevant topics.

Introducing AIMS Science Core Curriculum

Developed in alignment with your state standards, AIMS' Science Core Curriculum gives students the opportunity to build content knowledge, thinking skills, and fundamental science processes.
- *Each* grade specific module has been developed to extend the AIMS approach to full-year science programs.
- *Each* standards-based module includes math, reading, hands-on investigations, and assessments.

Like all AIMS resources these core modules are able to serve students at all stages of readiness, making these a great value across the grades served in your school.

For current information regarding the programs described above, please complete the following:

Information Request

Please send current information on the items checked:

_____ *Basic Information Packet* on AIMS materials   _____ Hosting information for AIMS workshops
_____ *AIMS Instructional Leadership Program*   _____ AIMS Science Core Curriculum

Name _____   Phone _____

Address_____
        Street   City   State   Zip

© 2002 AIMS Education Foundation

AIMS Publications

Actions with Fr
Awesome Additio
Bats Incredible! 2-
Brick Layers II, 4-9
Chemistry Matters, 4-
Counting on Coins, K-2
Cycles of Knowing and G
Crazy about Cotton, 3-7
Critters, 2-5
Down to Earth, 5-9
Electrical Connections, 4-9
Exploring Environments, K-6
Fabulous Fractions, 3-6
Fall into Math and Science, K-1
Field Detectives, 3-6
Finding Your Bearings, 4-9
Floaters and Sinkers, 5-9
From Head to Toe, 5-9
Fun with Foods, 5-9
Glide into Winter with Math & Science, K-1
Gravity Rules! 5-12
Hardhatting in a Geo-World, 3-5
It's About Time, K-2
It Must Be A Bird, Pre-K-2
Jaw Breakers and Heart Thumpers, 3-5
Looking at Geometry, 6-9
Looking at Lines, 6-9
Machine Shop, 5-9
Magnificent Microworld Adventures, 5-9
Marvelous Multiplication and Dazzling Division, 4-5
Math + Science, A Solution, 5-9
Mostly Magnets, 2-8
Movie Math Mania, 6-9
Multiplication the Algebra Way, 4-8
Off the Wall Science, 3-9
Our Wonderful World, 5-9
Out of This World, 4-8
Overhead and Underfoot, 3-5
Paper Square Geometry:
    The Mathematics of Origami, 5-12
Puzzle Play, 4-8
Pieces and Patterns, 5-9
Popping With Power, 3-5
Positive vs. Negative, 6-9

rimarily Bears, K-6
marily Earth, K-3
arily Physics, K-3
ily Plants, K-3
Solving: Just for the Fun of It! 4-9
nal Reasoning, 6-9
ctions, 4-8
cience, K-1
Bubbles, 4-9
blem-Solving Strategies, K-1
lem-Solving Strategies, 2
, 4-9
12
ience, K-1

e Explorers, 5-9
, K-2
Water, 2-6
nse: Temperature, Air Pressure, and Wind, 4-5
r Sense: Moisture, 4-5
ter Wonders, K-2

Spanish/English Editions*
Brinca de alegria hacia la Primavera con las
    Matemáticas y Ciencias, K-1
Cáete de gusto hacia el Otoño con las
    Matemáticas y Ciencias, K-1
Conexiones Eléctricas, 4-9
El Botanista Principiante, 3-6
Los Cinco Sentidos, K-1
Ositos Nada Más, K-6
Patine al Invierno con Matemáticas y Ciencias, K-1
Piezas y Diseños, 5-9
Primariamente Física, K-3
Primariamente Plantas, K-3
Principalmente Imanes, 2-8

*   All Spanish/English Editions include student pages in Spanish and
    teacher and student pages in English.

Spanish Edition
Constructores II: Ingeniería Creativa Con Construcciones
    LEGO® 4-9
    The entire book is written in Spanish. English pages not included.

Other Science and Math Publications
Historical Connections in Mathematics, Vol. I, 5-9
Historical Connections in Mathematics, Vol. II, 5-9
Historical Connections in Mathematics, Vol. III, 5-9
Mathematicians are People, Too
Mathematicians are People, Too, Vol. II
What's Next, Volume 1, 4-12
What's Next, Volume 2, 4-12
What's Next, Volume 3, 4-12

For further information write to:
AIMS Education Foundation • P.O. Box 8120 • Fresno, California 93747-8120
www.aimsedu.org • Fax 559.255.6396

Demco, Inc. 38-293

Duplication Rights

Standard Duplication Rights

Purchasers of AIMS activities (individually or in books and magazines) may make up to 200 copies of any portion of the purchased activities, provided these copies will be used for educational purposes and only at one school site.

Workshop or conference presenters may make one copy of a purchased activity for each participant, with a limit of five activities per workshop or conference session.

Standard duplication rights apply to activities received at workshops, free sample activities provided by AIMS, and activities received by conference participants.

All copies must bear the AIMS Education Foundation copyright information.

Unlimited Duplication Rights

To ensure compliance with copyright regulations, AIMS users may upgrade from standard to unlimited duplication rights. Such rights permit unlimited duplication of purchased activities (including revisions) for use at a given school site.

Activities received at workshops are eligible for upgrade from standard to unlimited duplication rights.

Free sample activities and activities received as a conference participant are not eligible for upgrade from standard to unlimited duplication rights.

Upgrade Fees

The fees for upgrading from standard to unlimited duplication rights are:
- $5 per activity per site; and
- $25 per book per site;
- $10 per magazine issue per site.

The cost of upgrading is shown in the following examples:
- activity: 5 activities x 5 sites x $5 = $125
- book: 10 books x 5 sites x $25 = $1250
- magazine issue: 1 issue x 5 sites x $10 = $50

Purchasing Unlimited Duplication Rights

To purchase unlimited duplication rights, please provide us the following:
1. The name of the individual responsible for coordinating the purchase of duplication rights.
2. The title of each book, activity, and magazine issue to be covered.
3. The number of school sites and name of each site for which rights are being purchased.
4. Payment (check, purchase order, credit card)

Requested duplication rights are automatically authorized with payment. The individual responsible for coordinating the purchase of duplication rights will be sent a certificate verifying the purchase.

Internet Use

Permission to make AIMS activities available on the Internet is determined on a case-by-case basis.

• P. O. Box 8120, Fresno, CA 93747-8120 •
• aimsed@aimsedu.org • www.aimsedu.org •
• 559.255.6396 (fax) • 888.733.2467 (toll free) •